PSALM 119

GOD'S KEY TO UNLOCK SCRIPTURE

BY WES PICKERING

Psalm 119
God's Key to Unlock Scripture
Wes Pickering

Print ISBN: 978-1-7335737-3-3
ebook ISBN: 978-1-7335737-4-0

wespickering.com

In honor of my wife Hannah who taught me to treasure daily the presence of the Holy Spirit through the simple act of returning to Scripture every morning. Your daily encounters with Jesus carried the weight of a thousand sermons and made me hungry to study the Word. You showed me that there truly is fresh bread waiting for me every single day, as reliable as the sunrise. Thank you for your love and your shining example of true discipleship.

TABLE OF CONTENTS

PREFACE

God is a genius. Our magnificent Father is not only the mastermind all of creation, but He's also the inventor of love. He's the pioneer of peace. He's the originator of joy! Nothing about the world or how it works escapes His notice or catches Him off guard. Nothing has ever rattled Him. He never has an off-day. He's always prepared for absolutely everything.

Have you ever wished that God also gave you the means to be prepared for absolutely everything? He has. He's given us Himself through the sacrifice of Jesus. Jesus gives us the Holy Spirit, who makes it His mission to unify us with God, empower us, guide us in every circumstance, and reveal the mysteries of the world to us. God has also given us His Word. The Bible contains within its pages everything a person needs to live a life of love, hope, fulfillment, and adventure!

For many, however, reading Scripture is a daunting task. The Bible is a massive book. Where do you even begin? If you start in the Old Testament, you have to trudge through thousands of pages before you're introduced to the main character, Jesus. But if you start with the New Testament, you might miss out on important context that explains why Jesus did and said what He did. People have spent the last 2,000 years arguing and debating over the meaning of difficult passages, including scholars with much higher IQs than most of us. Have you ever read the same few verses over and over again and still had no idea what they mean? I certainly have.

Being the genius that He is, God left us a key that unlocks the mysteries of His Word. It's easy to find: if you try to open your Bible to the exact center, there's a good chance you'll land on it. It's the longest chapter in the Bible, spanning pages and pages, a whopping 176 verses. Psalm 119 is the magnum opus of the Psalms. It's the place in Scripture that talks the most about

Scripture. When we learn to take the truth found in Psalm 119 and apply it to our study of the rest of the Bible, suddenly the entirety of Scripture comes alive.

Why did God give us the Bible in the first place? Is it an instruction manual? A book of moral philosophy? An epic story of good and evil? A love letter? Scripture is all of these and more. It is the most intimate and passionate love letter, the pinnacle of literature, the most flawless philosophy, and yes, even an instruction manual.

Unlike most instruction manuals, however, the Bible doesn't simply contain facts and data. There are very few step-by-step processes. You won't find any wordless pictograms to decipher like the ones that told you how to assemble your Swedish bookshelf. Instead, you'll find parables, biographies, songs, poems, letters, allegory, prophecy, history, and law. Why did God write it this way? Why did God span thousands of years and dozens of authors with as many styles of literature to write the most important document in history?

God poured His brilliance into Scripture to help His children live increasingly connected to Him. As we connect to Him, we also learn how to connect to each other. To know Him, we need more than data. We need to know more than simply *what* God thinks but also *how* He thinks. What brings Him delight? What fills him with sorrow? What does He honor? What does He abhor? What does He value? What is worthless to Him? How does He think about Himself? How does He think about you?

We will need all of eternity to explore the heights and widths and depths of God's infinite splendor and complexity, but every journey must begin somewhere. A wise place to begin with God is with what He says about Himself, and the only place to find that is in the Scriptures. As we read, the goal isn't merely to learn about God but to be transformed by Him.

In Psalm 119, the psalmist demonstrates how to study and respond to Scripture, not by using academic rigor or religious obligation but through heartfelt worship, fervent prayer, and diligent practice. You don't need to be a theologian to understand the Bible, only to have a willing heart that puts to use what you find. The psalmist leads us through the Scripture as a mentor pulling back the curtain on his private journey with God.

I'm passionate about teaching the Bible. My journey with Jesus began early as the son of missionary parents who taught me both the poetic beauty and life-saving practicality of God's Word. I grew up watching the Gospel transform broken people, and it made me hungry to participate in connecting others to God. For the last decade, teaching Scripture has taken me everywhere from megachurches in suburbia to ramshackle huts in the jungle. I've sat with pastors and drug dealers, kindergarteners and doctoral candidates, CEOs and homeless moms, and I've found that the Bible has treasure to offer everyone. Are you ready to unlock it?

ALEPH

Psalm 119 is a masterwork of literature. Like all the Psalms, it was not written merely to be read as poetry but to be sung. Every stanza of the song begins with a different letter of the Hebrew alphabet, starting with א or "aleph." Unlike the vast majority of songs we hear on the radio or in church today, Psalm 119's primary purpose isn't to convey emotion but to educate. Long before the ABC song, Psalm 119 taught not only the alphabet but how to truly live. However, the composer doesn't just give us facts and rules to remember. He pours as much emotion into his educational hymn as Michael Bolton would, singing a love ballad.

Like most effective writers, the author starts with something to grab his audience's attention. He begins with a promise:

1   How happy are those whose way is blameless, who walk according to the LORD's instruction!

Right away, Psalm 119 blows up a lot of bad theology. The psalmist begins by promising happiness! This would be enough to get him ostracized and excommunicated from certain theological circles. Even though Romans 14:17 tells us that the Kingdom of God is "righteousness, peace, and joy," many Christians balk at the idea that God cares about their happiness. Some try to separate happiness and joy as two entirely different things, as if a joyful person should not necessarily expect happiness to be part of his disposition. However, thinking this way excuses grouchiness and cynicism while still claiming to possess the "joy" that Scripture prescribes to all believers. Granted, joy encompasses much more than the emotion of happiness, but here we see unequivocally that God cares about our happiness.

No one could argue that God wants people to disobey Him. Of course not. He wants everyone to walk blamelessly, as the verse says. Well, I've got good news! If you keep God's instructions, you will be happy. Hardships will come, pain and sorrow — most assuredly, but through it all, God has hidden happiness like buried treasure at the center of righteousness. Happiness is the natural result of right living.

2 Happy are those who keep his decrees and seek him with all their heart.

Sometimes saying it once isn't enough. So, the psalmist doubles down on happiness. This time, he tells us where to set our aim. Happiness might be the promised result, but the target is God Himself. Our goal is to know Him, to draw close to Him, and to please Him. This requires a measure of trust because seeking after God and keeping His decrees frequently looks like the opposite of what society says will make a person happy. But Scriptural wisdom is often completely upside-down from conventional wisdom. The question then follows: who do we trust more, ourselves or God?

3 They do nothing wrong; they walk in his ways.

God will never set you up for failure. People, however, routinely do. Have you ever had someone get angry with you for doing precisely what they told you to do? I have, and few things are more frustrating.

"How can you be mad at me when all I did was what you said you wanted?" The trouble is that humans sometimes think we know what we want, but reality is less appealing than anticipated when we get it. When expectations aren't met, it's easier to blame someone else than face our shortsightedness. *They* must have done something wrong because this isn't the result I wanted!

But God doesn't do that…not ever. It is impossible to sin if you walk in God's ways. Everything about God's instruction is morally perfect. Following His ways will never lead your feet astray.

4 You have commanded that your precepts be diligently kept.

Obeying God's Word requires intention. Diligence isn't something that just happens all on its own. It demands careful attention. Diligence gives readers a specific focus when studying Scripture and questions we can ask as we read the text: What exactly does God command me to do? What does he ask of my attitude? What things that I read about should I be putting into practice? Obedience to Scripture is not just what God suggests as a best course. It's what He commands.

This verse introduces us to God's sovereignty. A lot has been written on the sovereignty of God, some of it good, some of it wildly inaccurate. But what's important to know here is that God's sovereignty means that He has the right and authority to rule the universe however He sees fit. As the Sovereign Ruler of all creation, He could have chosen a myriad of different ways to govern. He could have created people who would never disobey and would mindlessly follow His commands without even questioning the premise. But clearly, that's not the government God chose. Instead, He created human beings to have inquisitive minds, heartfelt emotions, and even the ability to choose wrongly.

God sovereignly chose to give humans free will. Why? Because He's not a tyrant. Tyrants are only interested in compliance. God, however, is interested in relationship. That's not to say that God doesn't want or even command obedience, but He wants obedience to be the outworking of relationship. You can't have a relationship with a robot, not really. God isn't interested in mindless robots who follow His every whim. He wants true servants, disciples, friends, and lovers. He's looking for people who will obey, not because they must, but because they trust and love Him.

5-6 If only my ways were committed to keeping your statutes! Then I would not be ashamed when I think about all Your commands.

Aha! Here is where the rubber meets the road, and the psalmist admits that this is all easier said than done. *If only I could keep your statutes!* Have you ever known the right thing to do but felt powerless to actually do it? You're not alone. That struggle is the plight of all human beings.

Verse 6 identifies a crucial symptom of disobedience: shame. Shame is a cancer that eats at the soul. Shame is the fruit that grows on the tree of knowledge without action. One of the primary definitions of sin in the New Testament is "to know the good and yet not do it" (see James 4:17). Like all fruits, shame eventually rots, containing within itself a seed that takes root in the soil of our hearts, and that seed grows more and more disobedience.

This is why Jesus died on the cross, to free us from the awful cycle of powerless disobedience and shame. In Christ, we are not only forgiven from the consequences of sin; we're empowered with Jesus' ability to live righteously. Where we were once powerless to obey God's commands, Jesus gives us His own capacity to obey. Jesus is the answer to the prayer: *If only!*

7   I will praise you with an upright heart when I learn your righteous judgments.

Many people are terrified of judgment, especially God's judgment. That's what shame does to us: it causes us to hide from God rather than run to Him for help. Do you remember what Adam and Eve did after the very first act of disobedience when they ate from the tree of the Knowledge of Good and Evil? They became ashamed and hid from God. God, for His part, had never given them any reason to be afraid of Him. Adam and Eve had only experienced God's amazing love and perfection. Why were they afraid of Him? Why not ask God for mercy, for help? Because sin distorts our view of who God really is, making our perspective like that of Satan's. Satan is terrified of God because he knows that one day he will face the ultimate judgment.

As believers, we finally have rest from the fear of judgment that plagues the world. We get to place all our shame and anxiety on the strong shoulders of Jesus. He carried it all and nailed it all to the cross. His perfect love completely expels every fear (see 1 John 4:19).

Verse 7 tells us a lot about the true nature of God's judgment. It is entirely righteous. God's judgment will never be unjust. There will never be anything unfair about the way God handles any situation, and all of His actions are worthy of praise.

There might come a time when it's difficult to see the fairness in God's judgment. Indeed, many passages in the Old Testament challenge our thinking about what justice truly looks like. But this verse lets us know that all God's judgments are opportunities for praise.

Sometimes, praise is an act of faith, choosing to trust that God is perfectly righteous and fair, despite the appearance of current circumstances. When we allow doubt to stifle our praise, we rob God of honor that He's worthy of. However, when we respond with praise to what we don't understand about God, we align our hearts to His true nature, and this is a profoundly solid foundation to build on.

When you don't know what to do, you can't go wrong with praising God. After all, we already have the promise that God's ways will yield happiness. Regardless of the circumstance, we can praise because we are guaranteed that God's outcome will always be good.

8   I will keep your statutes; never abandon me.

Notice that throughout this first stanza, the psalmist uses multiple synonyms for God's Word: instruction, decrees, precepts, statutes, commands, and judgments. When you read the Bible, take note of the ways the authors choose their words. Each of these words carries nuance, offering new vantage points, like holding a diamond at different angles to catch the light. The Bible can be read for the big picture, and it can also be studied in limitless depth for detail.

The first section of Psalm 119 concludes with resolve. I will obey. I will keep God's statutes. When we approach Scripture with the predetermination to obey, we can rest assured that God's empowerment will be with us. Not only that, but as we saw earlier, the end result is happy living!

The prayer, "Never abandon me," is a beautiful one and one that God loves to answer. All throughout the rest of Scripture, we read God's answer to that prayer. He will never leave us or abandon us. He is with us now and into eternity.

KEYS FOR STUDYING SCRIPTURE

1. Look for God's instructions and diligently put them into action.

2. Know that all God's decisions are morally perfect.

3. In any situation, praise is always the right response.

ב
BETH

When reading the Bible, one of the early challenges can be knowing what you're looking for. Should you read as you would a history book, learning lessons from people in the past? Is it a book of moral philosophy and high ideals? Is it God's biography that we might get to know Him? Without a doubt, Scripture contains all of these facets. However, God did not give us His Word merely for intellectual knowledge. Knowing is not enough on its own, for if my actions don't line up with what I know, the knowledge is worthless. As we read in the last section, knowledge without action always leads to shame.

9 How can a young man keep his way pure? By keeping your word.

Purity is vital because sin's contamination ruins us entirely. Sin is fatal in every instance. There is no such thing as a mild case of sin. It's impossible to keep it quarantined. Sin always spreads and always leads to death.

God's Word is the only reliable roadmap to purity. Obviously, we know that no one is capable of purity or moral perfection on his own, but Christ Jesus has gifted us His perfection for every place we've fallen short.

10   I have sought you with all my heart; don't let me wander from your commands.

Notice that the psalmist continually responds to God's Word with prayer. This is a necessary practice if we want to experience the promises found in Scripture. We all have a tendency to wander, but God delights in answering this prayer. The Holy Spirit gives us supernatural grace to obey God's commands. God Himself is our destination, and His Word is what keeps our compass pointed true north.

11   I have treasured your word in my heart so that I may not sin against you.

Sometimes temptation's pull seems irresistible, but let me assure you that it is not. God will never allow Satan to tempt you beyond your ability to resist (see 1 Corinthians 10:13). He always provides a way out. We find those escape routes by treasuring God's Word.

The Bible is more than a troubleshooting guide. As a matter of fact, if you wait until there's a crisis to turn to God's Word, you will more than likely fail to keep it. It's not enough to store the Word on your bookshelf; you must treasure it in your heart. When we value the Word enough to ponder it, memorize it, and store it up in our hearts, it brings us the necessary strength to fend off temptation.

12   LORD, may you be blessed; teach me your statutes.

Mingled with his prayer, the psalmist constantly praises and worships God. This is an exchange! As we seek knowledge and empowerment from God, we give love and affection back to Him. Oh, how beautiful the economy of Jesus is!

It's impossible to truly understand God's Word without the Holy Spirit's help. He is the ultimate Teacher. Jesus warned the Pharisees that they didn't know the Scriptures or God's power (see Matthew 22:29). This was an odd indictment because the Pharisees were the foremost Bible scholars in their day. Most of them had massive swaths of Scripture memorized. However, without God's powerful help, the Scriptures will yield no harvest.

There are plenty of "Bible scholars" today who don't even profess belief that Jesus is the Son of God. Their academic knowledge of Scripture provides them no benefit whatsoever. This isn't to say that scholarly understanding of Scripture is worthless. However, intellectual knowledge of the Scripture is only valuable so long as it draws one deeper in love with and obedience to God.

The Holy Spirit delights in being our Helper and Teacher. A request for His help is a prayer He is always ready to answer.

13   With my lips I proclaim all the judgments from your mouth.

Whatever comes off of God's lips is supernaturally powerful. He created the entire universe by speaking it into existence. One of the most profound acts we can participate in is to partner with God in proclaiming His judgments.

Whenever I'm faced with a problem, I always try to find God's solution in Scripture, and then I declare that answer as prayer over the circumstance. For example, if I'm battling illness, I declare Psalm 103:3 as my prayer: "You forgive all my sin, and you heal all my diseases." If I'm worried for a loved one who isn't following Jesus, I turn 2 Peter 3:9 into my prayer: "God, it's not your will that my loved one should perish in sin but that all would come to repentance. So, draw them into repentance."

I cannot begin to describe to you the power of declaring God's Word out loud. This doesn't mean that you deny the facts of your situation, but God's Word is the ultimate Truth. When you begin to declare the Truth over your circumstance, the facts will change.

14   I rejoice in the way revealed by your decrees as much as in all riches.

Scripture isn't just empty philosophy. It really works. When you begin to see how effective God's Word is at handling any situation, it becomes easy to value it above whatever the world has to offer. Seeing the Word in action is a continual opportunity to learn about God's character. He is immeasurably good! The breakthrough He brings to every situation is worth celebrating!

15   I will meditate on your precepts and think about your ways.

What do you think of when you hear the word "meditate"? If what comes to mind is a person sitting cross-legged droning, "ohhmmmm," you're probably thinking of what eastern religion calls meditation. The core of eastern meditation is to empty oneself of thought and emotion. At best, eastern meditation is a temporary distraction, but at worst, it's a dangerous gateway to dark spiritual forces who are attracted to empty vessels.

Biblical meditation, however, is entirely the opposite. Here we see that meditation means that we fill our minds with the Word of God; we ponder it and chew on it. Meditating on Scripture means that we allow the Holy Spirit to continually bring passages to our minds. As we do, we process its meaning, what it tells us about God, and how to put it into practice.

All serious reading is re-reading. Both C.S. Lewis and G.K. Chesterton argued that it's impossible to fully understand any text in the first read. Reading the Bible is not a one-time task to check off your list. It is an invitation to a lifetime of study and practice. The more we dig, the more we discover.

16   I will delight in your statutes; I will not forget your word.

Many Christians will readily admit that they don't enjoy reading the Bible, but God has actually hidden delight like buried treasure inside it. Every challenge we face in life is an opportunity to dig up God's riches. Within the storehouses of His Word, God has deposited more than enough supply for every need we will face.

Whenever I leave the house, I automatically check to make sure I have my phone, keys, and wallet. Forgetting any one of these things can ruin my plans for the day. But God's Word is more valuable and useful than everything I carry daily put together.

Psalm 119

Journeying through life without it is fraught with peril, but keeping it close as guidebook and compass will yield unending delight.

ב beth

KEYS FOR
STUDYING
SCRIPTURE

1. It's impossible to understand or obey Scripture without the Holy Spirit's help.

2. Meditating on Scripture prepares us for life's challenges.

3. Turning Scripture into prayer invites God's solution to any problem.

4. Reading the Bible is not a one-time experience. The more we re-read, the more treasure we uncover.

ג
GIMEL

iving by God's standards has always been counter-cultural. Throughout Scripture, you'll see God continuously calling His people to live to a higher standard than the world around them. From the Ten Commandments to the sermon on the mount to the apostles' letters, God consistently draws people closer and closer to His love and His Kingdom. But it isn't easy. Living God's way might be the most costly decision of your life!

17 Deal generously with your servant so that I might live; then I will keep your word.

History contains countless stories of valiant men and women who refused to cave when the world pressured them to compromise, even when their stand came at a great price. The pages of Church history are full of martyrs who paid the ultimate price when the world demanded they abandon God's ways. But those who trust in God have double assurance. Not only do we have a God who deals generously with people in this temporal life, but He has also removed the fear of death for all those in Christ. Confidence in God's generosity is what empowers believers to keep the Word.

18   Open my eyes so that I may contemplate wondrous things from your instruction.

What happened when Jesus gave instructions? The sick got up from their beds. Blind eyes opened. Food multiplied. Peter walked on water. From "let there be light" to this very moment, as you read this book, God's Word has never ceased to be miraculous. If we ask Him to illuminate His instruction to us, we will begin to experience His wonders.

If God instructs it, we can be sure that it's for our good. Even if His instructions seem burdensome or costly, His economy always works in our favor when we participate. When He asks the impossible of us, we can be certain that His Word contains within itself the power to get the job done. With God, nothing is impossible. Our part is to trust and obey.

19   I am a resident alien on earth; do not hide your commands from me.

This world we live in is rapidly passing away. Time is finite and will come to an end. In Christ, we are citizens of an entirely different universe, one that is eternal. Our loyalty is first and foremost to God's Kingdom, and our rights and privileges all originate with Jesus. The temporal earth is not our home. Therefore, we hold the things of this world very loosely: our possessions, our ambitions, and even our lives. Compared to eternity, even a thousand years on earth is mathematically zero. This life is a blip, a vapor.

Not only are we "resident aliens" in this world, but we're also ambassadors of our true home. God commissioned us to have everything we say and do represent the eternal Kingdom of Heaven. That's why Jesus taught the disciples to pray, "Your Kingdom come, Your will be done—on earth as it is in Heaven." We are legally designated representatives of His world.

Every commandment that God gives comes from His throne, His seat of authority in Heaven. As we follow those commands, we participate in the reign of God's Kingdom and are unshackled from the slavery of the kingdoms of earth. God's rules supersede the world's rules, and things in the Kingdom of Heaven don't work the same way the earth does. To live, you must lay down your life. To receive, you must give. To understand, you must become like a child. To win, you must surrender. Once you've genuinely experienced His world, you won't want to return to "normal."

20   I am continually overcome with longing for your judgments.

Once again, the theme of judgment comes up, and again it begs the question: why would someone long for judgment? Because God's judgments are designed to benefit us, His sons and daughters. Outside of Christ, judgment is a terrifying prospect indeed. But in Him, everything about His Kingdom works in our favor. He no longer remembers your sin because Jesus eradicated it. God judges you righteous. Even God's wrath works in your favor because He is furiously opposed to anything that would harm you. All of Satan's work against you—sickness, poverty, family strife, abuse, tyranny, trauma, anxiety, depression, etc.—all of these are grave injustices because Jesus already paid the fine for the sins of the world. Jesus is now our legal advocate, and God is a just Judge. All of His judgments bring life and liberty to those who follow Jesus.

21   You rebuke the arrogant, the ones under a curse, who wander from your commands.

From the moment Adam and Eve disobeyed and ate the forbidden fruit, the earth became subject to sin's curse, but Jesus died to reverse that curse. In Him, we have access to total freedom. However, many Christians don't walk in the liberty He affords us. Disobeying God is like voluntarily placing yourself under a curse. Obedience is not about rule-keeping: do this—don't do that! It's about recognizing that Jesus gave us righteousness as a gift. Rejecting that gift is foolish and arrogant.

Imagine living in prison for 40 years on death row. Execution day has finally come, but at the last moment, the President grants you a full pardon. However, instead of walking out of jail as a free person, you decide, "I'll stay here for a while…it's what I'm used to." That's precisely what we do when we carry on living in disobedience.

The Apostle John wrote in his first letter to the Church, "My little children, I'm writing to you so that you may not sin." He's not trying to *convince* us not to sin. He's letting us know we don't have to anymore (see 1 John 2:1)!

On the other side of the coin, when somebody sins against us, we don't have to be afraid or seek retribution. God's rebuke will deal with them. Our struggle isn't with other people but with the unseen forces of darkness that influence human behavior (see

Ephesians 6:12). Our role is to be ambassadors of the light, drawing people out from under the curse of darkness. There's no reason to live under a curse any longer, not for you, not for anyone!

22   Take insult and contempt away from me, for I have kept your decrees.

Living God's way isn't always easy. You will be misunderstood, wrongfully accused, and insulted. But don't be discouraged. We have exchanged the temporary discomforts of this life for the eternal bliss of the Kingdom of Heaven. Jesus told His disciples, "In this world, you will have trouble, but take heart! I have overcome the world!" (See John 16:33)

23   Though princes sit together speaking against me, your servant will think about your statutes;

God's law says that those who have entrusted their lives to Christ do not need to fear slander or any harm. When the world ratchets up the pressure, we stay focused by remembering the Word. Keeping the promises of God at the forefront of your memory will make you bold in the face of opposition, gentle in the face of persecution, and fearless in the face of death.

24   your decrees are my delight and my counselors.

There is no wisdom greater than God's. For every challenge that comes your way, God has a brilliant solution. Studying the Bible will help you implement His genius into your daily life. A good counselor doesn't just tell you *what* to think but teaches you *how* to think. The Word and the Spirit are the very best counselors. Every delight of God's Kingdom is up for grabs. All you have to do is learn to think like He does.

KEYS FOR
STUDYING
SCRIPTURE

1. In Christ, all of God's judgments work in your favor.

2. God's Word carries the power and authority of Heaven to affect change on earth.

3. Hanging on to God's promises will give you strength to face any opposition.

DALETH

What happens when life doesn't seem to line up with what God promised in the Word? It's an experience that every Christian will have sooner or later. Where is that happiness Psalm 119:1 promised? Where is the healing of 1 Peter 2:24?

John the Baptist had a moment like this as he sat locked in a prison cell. He knew the prophecies of Isaiah: that the Messiah would heal the lame, give sight to the blind, open deaf ears, and set the captives free. But if the Messiah was supposed to set the captives free, why was he still rotting in a prison cell?

Growing discouraged, John sent word to Jesus and asked, "Are you really the Messiah, or is there someone else we should be waiting for?" Jesus responded by turning to the crowd of sick people who were gathered and healing them. The lame walked, the blind saw, the deaf heard! But what about the captives? What John didn't realize was that Jesus came to do more than set people free from physical prisons. He was about to destroy the prison of sin and death for all who believe in Him. And yes, He literally sets captives in jail free too (see Acts 5, Acts 12, and Acts 16).

Sometimes it's easy to keep a ledger of what we see and what we don't see, what's good and what's bad. Something good happened today: so, that's one tally in the good column. Two bad things happened today: so, that's two tallies in the bad column. Living by what we experience requires no faith, and sooner or later, that road leads to destruction. Simply put, faith is trusting the information you have enough to act on it. Faith grabs ahold of the promise and doesn't let go until it comes to pass. When circumstances dictate your thinking, words, and behavior, your life will ultimately be unstable. But when you anchor your behavior in faith, circumstances will come and go, and you will remain steady. Which pathway will you choose?

25 My life is down in the dust; give me life through your word.

Scripture never portrays a cleaned-up, rose-colored, unrealistic version of life. Here you will find the entire spectrum of human emotion, from euphoric joy to crushing despair. Through it all, you'll discover God meeting His people right where they are, constantly pulling them deeper into His embrace. The Word contains life for every situation that's down in the dust. God has a way of gathering the dust and breathing life into it.

26 I told you about my life, and you answered me; teach me your statutes.

Doesn't God know everything already? Why would you tell God about your life? Of course He knows everything, but that doesn't mean He's disconnected from your story. Remember, God is relational. Not only will He listen when you bring Him your struggles, but He will also give you a timely answer. His answer always contains exactly what you need to overcome. Once we've experienced God's solutions to our problems, we should only be hungry for more.

27   Help me understand the meaning of your precepts so that I can meditate on your wonders.

Any understanding of Scripture that doesn't include the miraculous is either incomplete or inaccurate. Here, the psalmist indicates that understanding God's Word directly leads to observing His wondrous acts. While it isn't difficult to find a Bible scholar who dismisses the miraculous altogether, defending such a position with what the text of Scripture actually says is impossible. From start to finish, the Bible expounds on God's miraculous goodness and promises that He never changes His nature.

Rather than ignore the supernatural acts of God or write them off as irrelevant to our lives, we should meditate on them. We should ponder what miracles indicate about God's goodness. We should allow the testimony of miracles to increase our faith. God has never stopped being miraculous. Jesus is still the wonder worker!

28   I am weary from grief; strengthen me through your word.

Satan cannot defeat you, not on his own anyway. This is because Jesus already won total victory over Satan when He died on the cross and rose from the grave. However, Satan can try to wear you down, hoping that you will lose faith and give in. That's why the Apostle Paul instructs us to arm ourselves in defense of Satan's attacks, and once we're armed, we stand our ground (see Ephesians 6:10-18). Standing isn't always easy, but God promises to give you strength. He is not aloof to your pain and has embedded His power into His Word. God's strength will always outlast and overcome the enemy. Even at your weakest moment, He will not fail you if you keep your trust in His Word.

29 Keep me from the way of deceit and graciously give me your instruction.

What is the way of deceit? It is the world's way of doing things. Jesus described Satan as the "father of lies," and deceit is his native tongue. Every pathway outside of God's instruction is a lie, and deceit ultimately leads to destruction. But God has graciously given us the path back to wholeness.

30 I have chosen the way of truth; I have set your ordinances before me.

You have a choice as to what gets your attention. What things influence your thoughts and behavior? You can choose to give your recognition to movies, money, sex, social media… Every day, there are thousands of things vying for your attention. The things you think about, whether consciously or unconsciously, have tremendous influence over your behavior. The Apostle Paul warns in Romans 12 not to conform to these patterns of the world. We can't afford to think the way the world thinks.

Thinking the way God thinks will transform every aspect of your life, but learning to think God's thoughts doesn't happen automatically. We must choose to set God's ordinances in our view and keep them there. There will always be temptation to divert your eyes elsewhere, but steady focus on God's ordinances will keep you on the right path. A GPS navigation system can't guide you without a signal from the satellite. God's Word is our fixed anchor point, our satellite, that will guide us all the way home.

31   I cling to your decrees; LORD, do not put me to shame.

The journey will at times be turbulent. At times you may feel like all hope is lost, but don't lose your grip on the Lord's promises. Cling to them with all your might, and do not yield.

As Jesus hung on the cross, people stood around Him mocking. If this was the Savior of the world, why couldn't He save Himself? Hebrews 12:2 says that Jesus "despised the shame" and endured the agony of the cross. How did He do this? By remaining focused on "the joy that lay before Him." For Jesus and for you, joy is found in page after page of God's promises. Jesus knew that his mockers would not have the last laugh. He steadfastly clung to the Father's decrees and broke the power of shame forever.

32   I pursue the way of your commands, for you broaden my understanding.

It's not enough to pursue the *knowledge* of God's commands. We must pursue *the way.* As a matter of fact, the early Christians in the book of Acts are called "followers of the Way." Beyond mere intellectual ascent, God's commands require action.

Just as reading a book about Switzerland is not the same as packing your bags and moving to Switzerland, the Kingdom of Heaven is much more than what you know. It all hinges on what you do. We must live in the Kingdom, not just be educated about it. Knowledge about God is essential, but without action, it's worthless. That's why the Apostle James tells us that "faith without works is dead" (see James 2:17).

Don't settle for dead faith. Grab ahold of God's promises and walk them out with your actions. Along the way, God will broaden your understanding, opening your eyes to His Truth.

KEYS FOR
STUDYING
SCRIPTURE

1. God is not indifferent to our pain, and He listens when we bring our troubles to Him.

2. God's strength is always available to us through the Word.

3. Keeping the Word of God as our focus yields miraculous transformation, both of ourselves and our circumstances.

ה

HE

What's the first thing that comes to mind when you hear the word "obedience"? How about the word "submission"? For many, these words feel prickly and uncomfortable. Often, they come with negative, even painful connotations because of how we have experienced them in the past. However, the truth about God is that He is so profoundly good that submission and obedience to Him are actually full of joyous liberty. In the Kingdom, submission is never degrading or weakening. On the contrary, strength and dignity are impossible to obtain *outside* of submission.

33-34   Teach me, LORD, the meaning of your statutes, and I will always keep them. Help me understand your instruction, and I will obey it and follow it with all my heart.

God will never give you a command without giving you the strength and ability to obey it. He has embedded the power to succeed inside of your submission and obedience. If God has assigned it to you, be assured that He has empowered you to accomplish it fully. Don't think that God won't ask you to do something that's beyond your own ability…He certainly will! But He will empower you with *His* ability when you've reached the end of yours.

As you seek to understand God's commands, you will find greater and greater resolve to keep them. All of God's commands point back to His goodness. Understanding a command is the same as discovering another facet of God's perfection, and everything we discover about God is another opportunity to worship Him.

35   Help me stay on the path of your commands, for I take pleasure in it.

Sometimes, one of God's commands might seem unappealing or even offensive. I've actually heard Christians say, "I hate that verse!" about a particular Bible passage that struck a tender nerve. The Bible has lots to say about sex, sobriety, marriage, money, and virtually every other hot-button issue you can think of. Along the way, there's bound to be something that causes your alarm bells to go off, and you'll likely feel your emotional fight or flight response kick in. But if you "hate" a verse in the Bible, I can guarantee you that you don't fully understand it.

Many Christians are afraid to sincerely pray for God's will to be done in their lives because they suspect that God will want something for them that they don't want for themselves. They're terrified that God might ask them to do something excruciating or demand they eliminate something they love from their life. However, this line of thinking reveals a fundamental distrust of God's nature. Following through to its natural conclusion, one must believe that either God is not entirely good or that their plans are somehow better than His. Neither of these is accurate, not even remotely.

Undoubtedly, there is much about God and His plans for you that requires you to act in faith, pulling you entirely out of your comfort zone. Sometimes this might be a harrowing experience, as the old man's fleshly habits die in favor of God's new and better creation. However, the path God marked out for you is a pleasurable one if you follow it faithfully. Satan may interject with theft, death, and destruction, but none of those is any match for the abundant life found in Christ Jesus (see John 10:10). When life's difficulties come, it's vital to recognize who your real enemy is, and it isn't God. God is always your helper and never your problem. He adds no sorrow to his blessings for you (see Proverbs 10:22).

36 Turn my heart to your decrees and not to dishonest profit.

The world promises shortcuts to happiness and wellbeing, but all of these are illusions. Scripture is here to help you distinguish what is true from what is false. When an old pattern of thinking tempts you to take a dishonest advantage, the Holy Spirit will prick your heart with truth from Scripture about the situation. This is why we must carefully store up the Word in our hearts. The world has many distractions to lure you off the path of right living, but God's Word will show you that they're all mirages.

37 Turn my eyes from looking at what is worthless; give me life in your ways.

Everything outside of God's ways is worthless. Satan competes for your attention because, eventually, you become like what you admire. He promises the good life, but everything he has to show you will rot you to death. Only Jesus brings life. Only Jesus is the Way.

38 Confirm what you said to your servant, for it produces reverence for you.

God receives honor from fulfilling His promises. You should never be shy about staking your claim on God's promises because He is glorified as the Truth every time He keeps His Word. The Lord has no intention of denying you something that He promises in Scripture. He is good and faithful at every turn. Our part is simply to believe every promise He makes and celebrate Him for every promise fulfilled.

39 Turn away the disgrace I dread; indeed, your judgments are good.

There is no disgrace for people who put their trust in God's Word. Disgrace comes solely from the enemy. It is nowhere in God's agenda for humanity. In Christ, we don't have to fear a disgraceful judgment. He took our disgrace with Him to the cross and left it behind in the tomb. For us, for all who accept the sacrifice of Jesus, He has only a good verdict.

40   How I long for your precepts! Give me life through your righteousness.

If it were all about how perfectly *you* could keep God's commandments, you would indeed be in grave danger. But God has always been full of love and grace. Verse 40 is an astonishing revelation about God's relationship to man, written as much as 1,000 years before Christ's birth. It's not based on your righteousness that God grants you life. It's based on His.

In the New Testament, we find that the promise of God's righteousness goes even further than the psalmist could have imagined. Jesus not only covers our unrighteousness, he obliterates it. He not only clothes us in His righteousness, He supernaturally imputes it to us, transforming our very nature. In Christ, you are no longer unrighteous. His perfection has been given to you freely, and He has begun the process of sanctifying every imperfection you've ever possessed. Jesus has given us His Word as a gift to wash every stained behavior, every tarnished thought pattern, and make you completely holy. God no longer identifies you as sinner but as saint. The new you, the real you, is entirely whole and completely alive.

KEYS FOR STUDYING SCRIPTURE

1. Truly understanding God's Word gives us the resolve to obey it.

2. If any part of Scripture seems less than perfect, rest assured that you don't yet understand it.

3. God receives honor when He keeps His promises and loves fulfilling His Word.

4. Jesus has gifted you His righteousness. Scripture helps you live it out.

1
WAW

The Word of God is a written legal certificate for God's grace and favor. It is God's will and testament. How do we discover the will of God? Contrary to what many think, God's will is not a nebulous and unknowable search. To discover it, we simply look to what He wrote in His Law for us. Satan is conniving and does his best to cheat you out of what God sovereignly decreed belongs to you, but the Word of God contains your legal case against him. The Bible is our highest law book, containing both your responsibilities and rights as a child of God and a citizen of the Kingdom of Heaven.

41 Let your faithful love come to me, LORD, your salvation, as you promised.

How can you know for certain that God will forgive your sins? Because God has made salvation His promise to anyone who places their trust in Jesus. There are no limits to His grace, no sins so objectionable that they can exhaust His mercy. God's love is faithful, extending beyond the boundaries of man's capacity to rebel. You are not the exception to His rule, for that is impossible. Salvation is more reliable than all the laws of nature, physics, and mathematics combined.

42   Then I can answer the one who taunts me, for I trust in your word.

Satan's taunts very often tempt us to consider our present circumstances as more reliable evidence than the Word of God. "How could God possibly be perfect if He would allow this tragedy to happen?" Have you ever had a thought like that? In his ever-cruel and malicious way, Satan lures God's children to question His Word, asking the same question He presented to Eve in the Garden of Eden: "Did God *really* say…?"

It can be very tempting to trust our experience more than Scripture because often what we can see with our own eyes doesn't seem to line up with what God said. Most of the time, we wouldn't immediately conclude that God is lying (we know better than that). However, doubts creep up on our thoughts in more subtle ways: "Maybe that's true for someone else, but not for me." "Maybe God used to do that kind of thing, but He chooses not to anymore." "Maybe I'm supposed to understand God's Word philosophically but not take it to be literally true." "Maybe God is real and created the world, but He's uninvolved in the day-to-day life of humanity."

Faith is not based on what you can observe with your eyes. Instead, faith grabs what is unseen from God's Word and pulls it into reality, refusing to let go. Everything in God's Kingdom operates on the basis of faith, and without it, there is no hope to live a righteous life that pleases God (see Hebrews 11). The New Testament defines sin only a small handful of times, and one of those definitions is Romans 14:23 in which Paul explains, "Everything that is not from faith is sin." When Satan tempts you to dismiss the promises of God, he isn't just hoping you'll miss out on something good; he's enticing you to sin.

Verses 41 and 42 of Psalm 119 give insight on how to respond when Satan taunts you into doubt. You can go to God and pray that His promises will be fulfilled. You have permission to bring God's Word before Him and tell the Lord, "Satan is tempting me to believe that this isn't true, but I'm clinging to this promise. Let it come to pass!"

43   Never take the word of truth from my mouth, for I hope in your judgments.

We've already seen the importance of treasuring God's Word in the heart and the necessity of putting it into action. Now, we discover a new way to engage with Scripture: to speak it out loud. There is tremendous power residing in the words that come out of your mouth. This is easily observable, even outside a religious context. People who continually speak negativity are more likely to struggle and fail, but people who speak hope and optimism are more likely to succeed. A child who is taught to say, "I'm stupid," will undoubtedly struggle in school, but the same child taught to say, "I'm smart," will be hungry to learn and thrive. Proverbs 18:21 says, "Life and death are in the power of the tongue, and those who love it will eat its fruit." Your spoken words are a powerful weapon, and they can either be a force for good or a force for evil.

One of the benefits of speaking the Word of God aloud is that it generates faith. Romans 10:17 tells us that faith is developed when we hear the Word of God. Your ears need to hear the truth from your lips. When you speak Scripture, you can know for certain that your words are true. Don't allow your lips to negate the hope God gives you. Agree with Him in what you say, and your faith will grow. Not only that, but you'll exercise the delegated authority Jesus gave to His disciples to advance His Kingdom into every territory the enemy is battling to occupy.

44   I will always obey your instruction, forever and ever.

It's time to throw out your Plan-B! Have you ever sung the hymn, "I Have Decided to Follow Jesus"? The disciple's life is one of no compromise, "no turning back." One of the most powerful prayers you can pray is, "God, I will obey no matter what." Hell trembles when one of God's children pledges undying, unconditional allegiance to Christ.

In March of 1519, Spanish conquistador Hernan Cortés made landfall on the coast of Mexico with 11 ships and over 600 men, intent on conquering the treasuries and territories of the Aztec empire. Others had tried and failed before him, but Cortés was determined to succeed or die trying. So, he did something unprecedented: he sank his ships. With all 11 vessels buried under the Caribbean Sea, he and his men canceled any options for retreat. The only way forward was to conquer, and conquer they did.[1]

Jesus issued a sobering warning to fair-weather followers in Luke 9:62: "No one who puts his hand to the plow and looks back is fit for the Kingdom of God." In other words, you can't expect to plow straight lines if your aim isn't straight ahead. Greatness is often stolen by failure to commit. In the Kingdom of Heaven, we do not have the option of having divided loyalty. Serving two

---

[1] "Hernán Cortés," Encyclopædia Britannica (Encyclopædia Britannica, inc., January 7, 2021), https://www.britannica.com/biography/Hernan-Cortes.

masters is unacceptable. If we want to live in the Kingdom, we serve King Jesus and none other.

Would you decide to take disobedience off the table? Do you resolve to obey God's instruction no matter what? If so, get ready for the wildest adventure of your life! You won't always get it right. Sometimes you'll try and fail, but willful disobedience must be a thing of the past. I have often prayed, "God, no matter what you ask of me, you have my unconditional 'yes' in advance. Just don't let me miss it!"

God is looking for loyalty. In the soil of a loyal heart, God plants miraculous things. The Kingdom of Heaven manifests in power for those who have chosen to obey God's laws. Obedience cannot have an expiration date. It's the only way forward, forever and ever.

45   I will walk freely in an open place because I study your precepts.

In 1947, the prevailing wisdom among pilots and engineers was that an airplane pushed beyond the speed of sound would tear apart under the force of the shockwaves. Every time a pilot approached 700 miles per hour, their aircraft would shake so violently that there seemed no other option than to slow down. But General Chuck Yeager carried the same kind of determination as Hernan Cortés. Figuratively speaking, General Yeager sank his ships, deciding to push his jet where none had ever gone before, and as he breached the sound barrier, the desert below shook with the force of the ensuing sonic boom. Much to everyone's surprise, Yeager found smooth skies on the other side of the sound barrier.

The violent resistance was gone, and he streaked across the sky effortlessly.[2]

Although following the laws of God may seem burdensome at the outset, what we find on the other side of obedience is liberty. God does not write laws to keep you in bondage but to set you free. Everything outside of obedience is bondage. James 1:25 promises that, to the obedient, God's law is liberty itself. Satan has no chain strong enough to keep bound the one who is obedient to God.

46   I will speak of your decrees before kings and not be ashamed.

God's law is a higher authority than any man-made government. Throughout history, many tyrants have tried and failed to contain the spread of the Gospel. Bold saints have stood without compromise or fear before kings who exalted themselves as gods. Obedient disciples of Jesus can stand without shame in the face of death because God's law of life extends beyond the realm of the natural. A tyrant can take your mortal life, but God's law is true even into eternity.

47   I delight in your commands, which I love.

Loyalty to God's commands will unshackle you from all the things that bind up the rest of the world. Fear, shame, depression,

Goldstein, Richard. 2020. "Chuck Yeager, Test Pilot Who Broke the Sound Barrier, Is Dead at 97." *The New York Times*, December 8, 2020, sec. U.S. https://www.nytimes.com/2020/12/07/us/chuck-yeager-dead.html.

anxiety, poverty, and even bodily illness cannot stand up to the power of God's perfect law. If you want to experience delight like no one else experiences, learn to obey like no one else obeys.

48 I will lift up my hands to your commands, which I love, and will meditate on your statutes.

Raising your hands is a physical act of worship and surrender. It's why you will often observe people at church raising their hands during the music. Like kneeling or bowing, raising your hands is a practical demonstration of loyalty and honor. Even Satan understands this concept. That's why when he tempted Jesus, he said, "Bow down and worship me" (see Matthew 4:8).

In the Kingdom of Heaven, symbolic physical acts can carry great power. For this reason, God instructed Moses to stretch out his staff over the Red Sea. It's why Jesus tells us to "lay hands on the sick." It's why we still eat and drink the bread and wine of communion. In God's world, there's no such thing as "purely symbolic." Symbolic acts can release real spiritual power.

So, in all things—your thoughts, words, and actions—let your response to God be obedience and worship. God deserves your whole heart. He really is that magnificent and good.

KEYS FOR STUDYING SCRIPTURE

1. The Word of God carries the legal authority of the Kingdom of Heaven.

2. In the face of opposition, turn the promises of God into prayer.

3. Every option outside of God's law is sin and leads to destruction.

ז
ZAYIN

W e began Psalm 119 with a promise of happiness to those who walk righteously. But what happens when the fulfillment of that promise is nowhere to be found? How should we respond when there appears to be a cavernous difference between what we're experiencing and what the Bible promises? What if our circumstances are the exact opposite of what the Bible says?

49 Remember your word to your servant; you have given me hope through it.

Once again, the psalmist returns to the theme of reminding God of His promises. Are we to assume that God is absent-minded and forgot what He said? Certainly not.

When we remind God of His Word, we align our hearts to the only trustworthy source of hope. Satan would love nothing more than to divert your hope away from the promises of God and onto something else. It's not only that Satan wants you to be heartsick but that he wants to steal your worship. 1 Peter 1:3 refers to Jesus as our "Living Hope." Hope is more than just an optimistic emotion; it's the presence of Jesus residing in our outlook. When we remind God of His promises, we aren't being entitled; we're actually worshiping our Living Hope.

50   This is my comfort in my affliction: Your promise has given me life.

Throughout life, afflictions will undoubtedly come, and every affliction is an opportunity to worship Jesus as the promise keeper and the giver of life. Fixing your eyes on Him will comfort your aching heart and pull you towards His breakthrough. Don't lose your faith in God's promise, for in the promise, there is life. Don't give in to the temptation to think of "life" as a metaphor. Remember, Jesus' words literally heal the sick and raise the dead. You don't have to deny reality in order to have faith; simply deny the circumstances influence over your faith and obedience. Whatever you're facing, Jesus is truer than your circumstance.

51   The arrogant constantly ridicule me, but I do not turn away from your instruction.

As much as verses like these give us guidance for how we should respond to trials, they also exist in Scripture as prophetic foreshadowing of Jesus. No one has ever exemplified the psalmist's words better than Christ Jesus on the cross. Surrounded by mockers who blasphemed Him, Jesus did not abandon His mission. Jesus humbled Himself and submitted totally to the

Father's instructions, even to His dying breath. Our great hope is that the same Holy Spirit who empowered Jesus' perfect obedience now lives inside us.

52 LORD, I remember your judgments from long ago and find comfort.

The Bible is full of assurances that God never changes. He is the same yesterday, today, and forever (see Hebrews 13:8). With that in mind, one of the best things you can do to bolster your faith is to recall the testimonies of how God moved in the past.

When your situation seems hopeless, bring to mind the many ways God has been faithful before, and know that He has not changed. If He did it before, He'll do it again. You can even celebrate the testimonies of other people, countless Christians throughout history, as evidence that God really is who He says He is. Recalling testimonies is a powerful component of your worship. We see the evidence of who God is in what He has done, and all of it is worthy of our praise!

53 Rage seizes me because of the wicked who reject your instruction.

Following the Way can be a lonely experience. Obedience to Jesus will necessarily lead you in the opposite direction of what many consider to be normal behavior. Popular culture has a nasty bent towards celebrating things God hates. We don't like talking about it much, but God's wrath is a Scriptural reality. God hates sin because of how it degrades His good creation and breaks the fellowship He desires with His children. In Christ, we are to love what God loves and hate what God hates. Humanity is the target of God's love, but sin receives the full brunt of His wrath.

The critical distinction here is that God never violates His own character, even as He furiously hates sin. How can you be sure to do the same? One simple guideline is to always stay within the boundary lines of the Fruit of the Spirit (see Galatians 5:22-26). Any expression of anger that violates love, joy, peace, patience, kindness, goodness, gentleness, faithfulness, or self-control steps outside the boundaries of God's character and is unacceptable for a Christ-follower. Be careful not to linger on anger. Ephesians 4 warns that anger that extends beyond a single day gives the Devil opportunity to pull your heart into sin. Remember that your enemy is not another person but Satan himself.

54   Your statutes are the theme of my song during my earthly life.

Don't forget that the entirety of Psalm 119 is a song! All of the Psalms are. Why do we spend so much time in church singing? Because God created music to move the soul (your mind, will, and emotions) in a way that nothing else can. When you sing about the Truth, you sow seeds of faith into your own heart. Have you ever noticed how music is always at the leading edge of culture? If you want the culture of your heart to look like the character of Jesus, make sure the songs that you sing and the songs that you listen to reflect His culture.

55   LORD, I remember your name in the night, and I obey your instruction.

You will spend about one-third of your life asleep, but God did not design wasted time into His plan for you. Rest is a vital part of life, both in the physical and the spiritual. However, when hardships come, one of the first things to get disrupted is sleep. How many nights have you spent lying awake with both rest and the answers to your questions eluding you?

The moments between laying your head on the pillow and falling asleep are an invitation to step into the presence of Christ Jesus. Notice that, in this case, the psalmist doesn't say that he meditates on what to do, what he got right, or what he got wrong throughout the day. He simply remembers the Lord's *name*. In other words, he ponders who God is. He recalls God's nature, His authority, and His power. Somewhere in the process of thinking about God, he finds himself empowered to continue obeying.

Instead of trying to figure out how to handle your situation, if sleep is evading you, try simply becoming aware of the presence of Jesus. He is right there with you, at every moment. In Him, you will find rest and the strength to face another day.

56   This is my practice: I obey your precepts.

Like all things in life, obedience to God requires continuous practice. When the situations of life test your resolve, don't abandon your practice. The more you practice, the more you will look like Jesus. When you read the Bible, look for ways to put what you're reading into practice.

How should you respond when life doesn't look like what Scripture promised? You keep practicing. Rest assured, God will be true to His Word, even if He has to move Heaven and earth. He never changes, and He's always good.

KEYS FOR
STUDYING
SCRIPTURE

1. Reminding God of His promises is an expression of trust and worship.

2. Look for Jesus everywhere in Scripture. Remembering Him empowers obedience.

3. Cling to God's character, even when the people around you do the opposite.

4. Shift the culture of your heart by singing the Scripture.

CHETH

The world's value system and Heaven's value system are not the same. Everything the world has to offer is temporary, but everything in Heaven is eternal. Remember, even if you lived to be 200 years old, mathematically, your life on earth would still be nothing compared to eternity. What you can obtain and accomplish on earth is a vapor, a blink.

The world values wealth, influence, status, and power as end goals, but in the Kingdom of Heaven, these are all just tools. Our end goal must be something entirely different, something that doesn't fade away when our time on earth is done...

57 The LORD is my portion; I have promised to keep your words.

God Himself is the goal. He is the portion we live for. His value is more significant than any amount of work we could ever accomplish. He is sufficient beyond any supply we could earn. In Him is the fulfillment of every dream, the supremacy of power, and the pinnacle of every ambition. There is nothing you could possibly need that you will not find in Him. He is all in all.

When honoring God becomes our highest goal, everything the world calls an ambition merely becomes a tool. If the tool is available, use it to glorify God. If not, glorify Him anyway! Do you possess wealth? Use it to build the Kingdom of God. Are you poor? Glorify Him with your little. Do you have power and influence? Use them to point others to Jesus. Are you a "nobody"? Obey God in obscurity, for He is your glorious audience of one.

All are capable of obedience and worship, from the highest ruler to the lowest slave. When God is your portion, you lack nothing.

58   I have sought your favor with all my heart; be gracious to me according to your promise.

Grace is God's promise. To obtain this promise, all anyone has to do is access it freely through faith in Christ. Accessing grace requires no means, no special talent, and no striving effort. Jesus earned the Lord's favor through His perfection, and He gives it to anyone who comes to Him.

On the other side of receiving grace, we have every reason to passionately pursue God's favor with everything we've got. While God has entirely given us Himself, He remains infinite in nature, and the more we seek His favor in response to grace, the more we discover of His goodness.

You have been plucked from the cold chains of tyranny and set down inside the gates of God's beautiful, free country. The Kingdom of Heaven is all free to explore, and it's too good not to. Journeying through God's Kingdom is a pilgrimage of limitless beauty, awe, adventure, and discovery. We seek God's favor, not to obtain Him, but because He has already completely given Himself to us. Instead, we seek His favor as a newlywed bride would her adoring groom, because we are madly in love!

59   I thought about my ways and turned my steps back to your decrees.

Occasionally, you will miss the mark. Although we have the perfect spiritual DNA of Jesus coursing through our veins, we're still infants learning to stand up on wobbly legs and walk righteously. Father God doesn't hate you when you wander off course. He gently calls you back, wooing you with His love and sometimes disciplining you for your benefit.

If an athlete has no discipline, he will fail to reach victory. No Olympian has ever reached the podium without great discipline and sacrifice. God's discipline isn't vengeful punishment but loving guidance and hopeful training, even when it feels difficult. He knows that you have the same athletic genes as Jesus, and He wants you to run the race as a champion. God's correction will never push you down into the mire. He will never address sin without giving you the grace to lift you out of it. His discipline always empowers us to succeed.

Christ is our example, our forerunner. Take an inventory of your life, and hold it up to His standard. Should you find your steps out of alignment with His ways, don't let shame keep you from turning your steps back to what God decreed. Shame tries to keep you from turning your heart to God's presence, but His presence is exactly what you need. Like the prodigal son, you will always find the Father running down the driveway to embrace you when you turn your steps towards home.

60   I hurried, not hesitating to keep your commands.

My mom used to tell me, "Slow obedience is no obedience." When you hear the command of the Lord, the quicker you obey, the less likely you are to disobey.

The longer you spend second-guessing, the greater your chance is of missing out on God's best for you. Many Christians struggle to hear God's voice, and one of the best ways you can tune your heart to discern is through obedience. When you're quick to obey, you'll begin to see the clear connection between your actions and God's favor.

As you read Scripture, try to find ways to put what you've read into practice as soon as possible. If I were to give you a baking lesson and teach you the process for making sourdough bread, the information would be yours to use from there on after. However, if you waited more than just a few short days, the likelihood that you'd remember the process and bake a loaf of bread on your own would get smaller and smaller.

Knowledge that isn't put into practice eventually fades away. Jesus warned us about this in Mark 4:24-25, "Pay attention to what you hear. By the measure you use, it will be measured to you—and more will be added to you. For whoever has, more will be given to him, and whoever does not have, even what he has will be taken away from him." Use it or lose it! Don't delay.

61   Though the ropes of the wicked were wrapped around me, I did not forget your instruction.

The pressure to compromise can be immense. All 12 of the Apostles died unimaginably cruel deaths as martyrs, with the exception of John, who died in exile on the island Patmos after every attempt to kill him failed. The disciples all clung to Jesus' instruction, and the life they found in Him could not be extinguished, even through the death of their mortal bodies.

Many Egyptian Christians tattoo an image of the cross on their wrists. In doing so, they've pre-decided that in the event that a persecutor threatens their life, they will not deny their loyalty to Jesus. That kind of faithfulness is what caused the Gospel to spread around the world like wildfire. If you have yielded your life to Jesus, you don't have to fear the wicked. Resolve to love Him with every moment you're alive, and the Holy Spirit will give you supernatural strength to overcome the fiercest power of hell.

62   I rise at midnight to thank you for your righteous judgments.

Have you awakened in the middle of the night and found it difficult to fall back to sleep? Don't allow anxiety to overwhelm you. Use the time as an opportunity for thanksgiving. It's virtually impossible to be anxious and grateful at the same time. At every moment, God is watching over you, pronouncing righteous judgments on your behalf.

63   I am a friend to all who fear you, to those who keep your precepts.

For too long, the Church has bogged herself down in conflict rather than strengthening the bonds of unity between brothers and sisters in Christ. There will always be opportunities to break fellowship, but we can't take that bait, for too much is at stake. God's blessing rests on those who stand unified under the banner of Jesus (see Psalm 133). Unity takes great effort, while discord will happen all on its own.

This isn't to say that legitimate disagreements on issues of theology and doctrine won't arise. There is an appropriate time to stand and defend the essentials of the faith. Sound doctrine is worth pursuing, and knowing the truth is crucial. However, we must be careful not to violate Scripture in our zeal to defend it.

John Wesley famously coined the term "agree to disagree" over the intense theological disagreements he had with evangelist George Whitfield. While they grappled with correctly interpreting Scripture, both Wesley and Whitfield wisely saw God's hand on the other. Both of them were used mightily during the First Great Awakening, leading thousands to Christ and bearing an impact that has lasted hundreds of years.[3] This doesn't mean that truth is relative, not remotely. It simply points to the generosity of God, who gives grace to us even while we don't yet fully understand.

In the New Testament, Jesus takes this call even further. In Matthew 11, Jesus refers to himself as the "friend of sinners." In Matthew 5, Jesus gives a new command to all who would follow Him: love your enemies. Now, we are called not only to be a friend to those who fear God but also to those who oppose Him.

How can we do such a thing? Because Jesus was a friend to us while we were still sinners. With His dying breaths, Jesus loved and forgave His murderers. Through the power of the Holy Spirit, we can show this same love to a broken world.

---

[3] "Wesley Vs. Whitefield | Christian History Magazine". 2021. *Christian History Institute*. https://christianhistoryinstitute.org/magazine/article/wesley-vs-whitefield.

ח **cheth**

64 LORD, the earth is filled with your faithful love; teach me your statutes.

The faithful love of God is what pulls a corrupt world out of darkness and into the light. God's kindness can draw the most rebellious person from mortal sin into a life of righteousness (see Romans 2:4). One of the primary ways that God desires to fill the world with His love is through His disciples. Jesus tells us in John 13:34-35 that love would be the primary identifier for His followers. By love, we will be recognized. The world is supposed to observe a purity in the way we love one another as the distinguishing mark of people who have chosen to follow Jesus.

Christians throughout the centuries have grappled with finding harmony in walking out the love of Christ and zeal for keeping His statutes. Some have emphasized the love of Jesus while excusing disobedience, yet others have stressed the necessity for obedience while neglecting love and mercy. In reality, righteous living and perfect love are completely harmonious with each other, and Jesus is living proof. He lived entirely righteously and preached the necessity of repentance, yet sinners of all kinds were attracted to Him because of His immense love. So many sinners wanted to be around Him that Jesus developed a bad reputation among the legalistic religious leaders. Still, He never once compromised the truth or failed to call those around Him to repentance and right living.

It is by love and for love that we obey, and we join the psalmist in his prayer, "Teach me your statutes." Through love, empowered by the Holy Spirit, we obey with all our hearts. The more we experience the love of God, the more we are pulled into Heaven's value system. As we align our values to God's, we begin to treat the people around us as valuable, and the earth is filled with the Lord's faithful love.

KEYS FOR
STUDYING
SCRIPTURE

1. Scripture teaches God's value system.

2. Repentance isn't shameful but a gift God gives us when we fall short.

3. The quicker we obey, the less likely we are to miss the mark.

4. God's love and righteousness are entirely harmonious. We must not abandon either.

TETH

od is good. How many times have you heard this? But do you really know what it means? That's probably a bit of a trick question because God's goodness can't possibly be put into words. Unspeakable joy, incomprehensible peace, and limitless love are all parts of God's goodness. Discipleship could be defined as discovering and yielding one's life to the goodness of God. In 1 John 1:5, our eyewitness apostle sums up the entire ministry and message of Jesus in one astonishing sentence: "God is light, and there is absolutely no darkness in Him." In other words, God is good, and there's nothing bad about Him.

65 LORD, you have treated your servant well, just as you promised.

Sometimes, we need to be reminded: God promises to treat us well. God will never withhold His goodness from you, nor will he ever do anything to you that is not good (see Psalm 84:11). Does that mean that we will never experience anything bad? Of course not. But it does mean that God is not the *source* of bad things. Sometimes we experience bad things because of our own choices, other times because of another person's bad choices, and sometimes simply because we have a real enemy in Satan who hates with his entire being. Whatever the scenario, remember, God is never your problem.

God is so powerful and good that no evil thing in this life will have the last say. Jesus' victory over evil is final, and when the totality of this time on earth is completed, no one will argue that the outcome is anything less than perfect. All will see clearly the magnificent goodness of God. But that doesn't mean God is waiting until later to be good. He is good right now, and He will be good to you at every turn. It's His promise.

66   Teach me good judgment and discernment, for I rely on your commands.

A huge part of experiencing the goodness of God and not crumbling under the enormous pressures of life is faithfully obeying God's commands. Failure to follow His commands leads to terrible consequences, not because God is vindictive, but because we didn't participate in the way God's world works. Everything outside of God's world is dysfunctional.

I recently gave some sourdough starter to a friend along with the recipe I use to bake bread. A few weeks later, she called and said, "I tried to make a loaf of bread, but it didn't rise."

I asked her to recount her process of preparing the dough, and she described combining the flour, water, starter, and salt. Then I asked, "Did you feed the starter before putting it into the dough?"

There was a long pause on the other end of the phone line. "No. I forgot to do that."

"That's why your bread didn't rise. You have to feed your starter with high-quality bread flour and water about 5 hours before you prepare your dough, and you have to keep feeding it at least once or twice a week for it to stay alive and healthy. That's the first step of the recipe."

Learning good judgment and discernment can be a lot like the process of learning to bake bread. The dough not rising wasn't a vengeful punishment for not following the recipe. It was simply the natural result of missing the step. The yeast in the starter is not vindictive. It simply has no means to grow without being fed.

Some of God's instructions have enormous consequences attached to them. God warned Adam and Eve well in advance, "If you eat from this tree, you will die." When they disobeyed, God didn't murder them as revenge for failing to keep His rules. Rather, God understood that living under His rulership is what connected them to the source of life. When Adam and Eve disobeyed, they exchanged God's rulership for Satan's. This is why Jesus referred to Satan as "the ruler of this world" in John 12:31. God never desired Satan to rule this world, and He gave specific instructions to prevent that from happening.

Thankfully, God has left nothing to chance, and our eternity is not hinged on how well we obey. Jesus obeyed to perfection, and our command is now to trust and follow Him. He earned for us what we never could on our own. Jesus reintroduces us to God's rulership and positions us to reap all the benefits of His obedience. For the disciple, obedience is now twofold. Firstly, we obey from love and honor in response to Jesus. Secondly, empowered by the Holy Spirit, we obey to participate in God's Kingdom and represent the King to the people who have not yet trusted in Him. Our obedience demonstrates to others that there is a better way, one that leads to eternal life and not death.

67   Before I was afflicted I went astray, but now I keep your word.

Because no one other than Jesus has ever lived without sin, we all experience the pain of our own disobedience. However, the longer you walk with Jesus, the more you will discover the beauty and joy of repentance. Repentance might feel painful in the moment, but its effect is nothing short of miraculous and wonderful. Repentance turns us away from the consequences of sin (ultimately, death) and reorients us into position to receive the benefits of God's goodness.

The first step in repentance is agreeing with God about the nature of our problem. Many wish to benefit from the Kingdom but refuse to agree with God about His standards for life. In essence, they want a Savior but not a Lord; but you cannot have one without the other. The Lordship of Jesus is what keeps us inside His protective power. The more we truly experience the freedom of God's way of life and the joy of connection with Him, the less pull our old patterns of behavior have on us.

68   You are good, and you do what is good; teach me your statutes.

If you can't find it in God's nature, it isn't good, no matter what anyone says about it. Goodness can be defined as moral perfection. Because God is morally perfect in both His character and actions, He has the right to define what is evil. A standard of living outside of His statutes might look appealing, but God knows better.

When we cling to something that God's Word forbids, we fundamentally slander His character. What we're really saying is,

"My understanding of morality is superior to God's, and therefore I will choose how to behave." Of course, most of us would never word it so bluntly, but all sin is the result of fundamentally distrusting God's goodness. In John 16:9, Jesus boils all sin down to simply not believing in Him. Believing in Jesus includes believing that what He says about life is true and acting on it.

Those who would claim that Scripture has been corrupted over time by humans and is therefore unreliable are essentially saying that God is not trustworthy enough to have preserved His Word and that they would have done a better job of it. Such thinking is sinking sand and leads a person into faith only in themselves and their own experiences. They find themselves committing Adam and Eve's sin all over again. "Did God really say...?" is a line that Satan loves and keeps using because humans keep falling for it.

God is good. Everything He does is good, and all of His statutes are good. There is nothing evil in Him and nothing good without Him. The natural result of trusting in God's goodness is hunger to know His statutes.

69   The arrogant have smeared me with lies, but I obey your precepts with all my heart.

Some people will fail to understand when you turn away from your sin and obey God. Jesus' disciples are frequently slandered, just as He was. Jesus was accused of blasphemy when He was the only one who truly honored the Father. He was reviled as a man controlled by demons when He was the one who set people free. He was ridiculed as a liar when He is the Truth.

A Godly lifestyle confronts those who are not fully surrendered. It's far easier to slander what's different about a disciple than admit that they're right and repent. But for those who have tasted and experienced God's goodness, there is no turning back. God is worth obeying fully because His ways are really that good.

70 Their hearts are hard and insensitive, but I delight in your instruction.

The simple lesson to learn here isn't thinking less of people who disobey. Instead, we should read this verse as a warning: disobedience eventually leads to hard-heartedness. Sin makes our spiritual ears insensitive to God's voice. If you want to experience the fullness of God's presence and have an ear that's fine-tuned to His voice, obey Him with delight!

71 It was good for me to be afflicted so that I could learn your statutes.

Did I mention that God is good? Everything He does is good. All of His plans and intentions towards you are good. His execution is always perfect. He has never missed the mark, not once.

Even when He disciplines us, God's goodness is perfect and uncompromised. God has never over-disciplined or under-disciplined. His discipline is always with your wellbeing at the forefront of His mind, knowing exactly what is necessary to keep you from harm. The corrective touch of His hand is never lighter nor heavier than absolutely necessary.

God knows what the stakes are: life, death, and eternity. While in the moment, discipline is almost never fun, over time, we always find that God's chastisement was the best possible course of action to keep us on the right path.

72   Instruction from your lips is better for me than thousands of gold and silver pieces.

The psalmist isn't writing from theory. It's apparent that he has life experience behind him. He has suffered the painful consequences of his own destructive actions. He has benefitted from the thoughtful discipline of a God who refused to let him go astray. He has witnessed the incalculable cost of sin, and it has become abundantly clear: God's instructions are priceless.

The goodness of God is a fundamental cornerstone of true theology. Without it, the rest of Scripture crumbles, leaving the reader to question whether God even exists at all. It's no accident that dozens of times throughout, Scripture plainly states, "God is good."

The great theologian A.W. Tozer wisely said, "What comes into our minds when we think about God is the most important thing about us."[4] When what comes to mind is God's goodness, it changes everything.

---

[4] A.W. Tozer, *The Knowledge of the Holy*. New York: Harper Collins, 1978.

KEYS FOR
STUDYING
SCRIPTURE

1. The goodness of God is a cornerstone of true theology.

2. All of God's laws are morally perfect and for our benefit.

3. God's discipline is designed to keep us from the grave consequences of sin.

> ׳

YOD

O verlapping Truth is a feature of Scripture. It's one thing to know that God promises to bless and protect the righteous (see Psalm 5:12). But that promise takes on a whole new level of meaning when overlapped with the revelation that those who put their trust in Jesus receive His righteousness as a gift (see 2 Corinthians 5:21). Together, these overlapping truths reveal that, on our behalf, Jesus unlocks all of the Bible's promises for the righteous, something we could never earn on our own.

At first glance, it's difficult to see where the psalmist is going in this section of Psalm 119. These eight verses seem to sandwich together a handful of ideas that have little to do with each other, but hang in there. Each verse can be examined by itself as true, but when viewed as a whole, a bigger, more important picture comes into view.

Throughout Scripture, you will occasionally find statements that seem at odds with one another, but the whole truth lies where the two overlap. Take, for instance, Jesus' famous beatitude, "Blessed are the peacemakers." What happens when we examine that next to one of Jesus' less prominent statements? "I did not come to bring peace, but a sword." Did something happen to Jesus between Matthew 5 and Matthew 10? No, Jesus is always and utterly consistent.

The Apostle Paul gives us crucial insight in Romans 12:18: "If possible, as far as it depends on you, live at peace with everyone." Not only is Jesus the world's foremost advocate for peace, He is peace itself. He is the Prince of Peace. Peace is much more than just an emotion or the lack of conflict, but rather the presence of Jesus Christ. Therefore, the goal of "blessed are the peacemakers" is not conflict-avoidance but the pursuit of God's presence and character in our relationships. Sometimes, however, peace with others isn't dependent on your actions. Jesus is the ultimate example here. While He perfectly embodied "peace on earth," not everyone on earth was at peace with Him.

Integrity holds fast onto what's right, even when it's costly. Sooner or later, following the ways of Jesus will bring conflict to your doorstep, and that day can be agonizing. People will misunderstand you, impugn your motives, and betray you; but when they do, you must fight the urge to fight back by their rules. "Turning the other cheek" sounds like noble advice, but it is easier said than done. When the pressure builds, we must hold fast to Jesus' example for how to respond. At times Jesus enjoyed the warm company of cherished friends, and other times He walked alone on a very narrow road.

73   Your hands made me and formed me; give me understanding so that I can learn your commands.

You do not belong to yourself. God is Creator of all, and everyone rightfully belongs to Him. That being true, He still loves you enough to let you reject Him. You may choose to be your own master, but doing so always leads to pain and destruction. God will even love you after you reject Him. However, there are moments in life that obfuscate this reality, when God's way seems illogical and even offensive. Faced with murky and competing ideals, we must remember that God is the reason for our existence. Everything starts and ends with Him.

Undoubtedly, choosing God's commands requires a leap of faith, but acknowledging Him as Creator brings what was once blurry into sharp focus. No amount of rebellion changes the fact that God made us, and we belong to Him. Who better to teach us the laws of the universe than the One who hung the galaxies in their orbits?

74   Those who fear you will see me and rejoice, for I put my hope in your word.

Not everyone will rejoice when you stand firm in Godly obedience. However, reverence for God includes joyful acknowledgment of His work in other people's lives. It is a mark of righteousness to celebrate those who put their trust in Jesus. All of this sounds easy enough, but putting it into practice is often challenging. When the world reviles a Christ-follower, embracing them can be costly.

75   I know, LORD, that your judgments are just and that you have afflicted me fairly.

The psalmist returns to the theme of verse 71 from the previous section: that even in affliction, God's goodness is on display. God never judges unjustly. However, it's important to note that whenever the psalmist repeats himself, the statement happens in a different context than before, and we are given a fresh angle from which to view the truth.

When read in the immediate context of the previous verse, both verses 74 and 75 take on fresh meaning. It's one thing to say that those who fear the Lord will rejoice when they see a brother walking in righteousness. But it's another thing to say that those who fear God will rejoice when he has experienced the just discipline of God. He's not talking about schadenfreude, the gleeful pleasure that people sometimes derive from watching another person suffer (perhaps because they deserved it). No, he's emphasizing that a Godly person rejoices when he sees someone with a repentant heart, even if that person is still in the middle of the mess they made. A righteous person rejoices when he sees God's goodness poured out on someone who doesn't deserve it!

Jesus, in perhaps His most famous parable, tells the story of a prodigal son returning. Upon seeing his wayward son in the distance, the loving father runs to welcome him and celebrate his homecoming. However, when the older brother hears all the commotion, he's disgusted to find out that their father is throwing a party for this brother who just finished squandering his inheritance on raucous, sinful living. But the father is adamant: we *must* celebrate when a sinner returns home (see Luke 15).

I'm sure the older brother had all the same excuses Christians have today. How do we really know if a person is repentant? After all, he has no good fruit growing from his actions. In fact, the only reason he came home is that he ran out of money. Why should we celebrate someone like that? Shouldn't we wait to see if their repentance is genuine? How do we know they're not going to blow it all over again?

76 May your faithful love comfort me as you promised your servant.

The unfailing promise of God towards us is unwavering love. His love persists even when everyone else's fails. When no one will give you another chance, God will. He extends mercy when everyone else seems to think you're getting what you deserve… even when you *are* getting precisely what you deserve. As disciples, we are to imitate God in showing mercy to those who deserve punishment, not with smug condescension but unwavering, tender love. God's judgment is always just, but mercy triumphs over judgment (see James 2:13)!

77 May your compassion come to me so that I may live, for your instruction is my delight.

Without God's mercy, we are doomed to suffer the brutal consequences of our sin. Each of us has earned death by our actions, but God in His compassion has given us eternal life (see Romans 6:23). Verse 77 is the voice of someone who has learned his lesson and come to true repentance.

Like George Bailey in the classic film *It's a Wonderful Life*, he has been given a new lease on life. Things he used to complain about are now precious. Difficulties he used to avoid are now opportunities to show devotion and gratitude. When you realize that God's love is what's keeping you alive, suddenly all of His instructions become delightful.

78 Let the arrogant be put to shame for slandering me with lies; I will meditate on your precepts.

At first glance, this verse isn't all that different than verse 69, but in the light of a new context, we're given a fresh opportunity to examine the message and examine our own hearts. Consider the contrast between this verse and what we just read in verse 74: the righteous person will see him and rejoice, but arrogant people slander. What's important to note is that he's already admitted that God was right to discipline him. So how can he call it slander if he knows he deserved discipline?

79 Let those who fear you, those who know your decrees, turn to me.

Those who know God's decrees understand that God is merciful and that He promises compassion and faithful love, but loving someone in the middle of their mess isn't always easy. Perhaps, like the psalmist, you've found yourself repentant but still in the middle of a mess. Even among disciples, it can be hard to shed the reputation of a sinner, despite your earnest repentance.

In the Book of Acts, Saul had his fair share of skeptics after he first repented, and who could blame them? He had been the worst persecutor of Christians until God confronted him, but now suddenly, he wants to join them in fellowship? There's no wondering why people questioned his motives (see Acts 9).

Distrust and suspicion of people's motives are rooted in fear. In Saul's case, the fear was palpable. Should they trust a man who had a reputation for imprisoning and murdering Christians? But

yod

often, people's fears are more subtle than that. What might embracing a prodigal cost? Will people view having mercy on a sinful person as a tacit endorsement of their sin? Will you fall victim to guilt by association?

Thankfully, the Kingdom of Heaven has citizens like Barnabas. In the Book of Acts, Barnabas had a reputation for embracing people that others rejected. He embraced Saul and introduces him to the Apostles. Later he embraced John Mark when Saul was furious at him for abandoning their missionary journey (see Acts 15). Praise God for Barnabas! For without his selfless embrace of the unlovable, we wouldn't have Paul's letters, nor would we have the Gospel of Mark. Those who have encountered the perfect love of Jesus cast aside all fear, including the fear of a damaged reputation for rejoicing over a prodigal's return home.

80   May my heart be blameless regarding your statutes so that I will not be put to shame.

The mercy of God doesn't just cover over a sinful heart and hide it from view. It completely renews the heart, blotting out all record that the sin ever occurred. With great compassion, God's grace transforms and renews a guilty person and makes them blameless. In Christ, you're more than just forgiven. Your record has been expunged as if you had never sinned in the first place.

This is why it's crucial that we embrace those who repent, no matter how vile their sin. How can we continue to keep a record of trespasses when God no longer does? 1 Corinthians 13 tells us clearly that to exhibit God's love, we are not permitted to keep record of people's wrongdoing. How could we forget the measure of grace and forgiveness God has given to us? Continuing to treat someone like a sinner after they've turned to God is arrogant and slanderous.

In Christ, you are not blighted by your sin. You are clean. Jesus has made you blameless, and He will not let you be put to shame.

KEYS FOR STUDYING SCRIPTURE

1. Overlapping truth emphasizes and clarifies even when two passages appear contradictory at first glance.

2. We do not belong to ourselves. As Creator, God has every right to give us instructions for life.

3. God's goodness and compassion are always present when He addresses sin.

כ
KAPH

When the fog of war settles on the battlefield, all the romanticism of being a soldier dissipates into harsh, ugly reality. It's one thing to know that Jesus said, "In this world, you will have trouble…" but another thing to be in the thick of trouble. Sooner or later, you will find yourself tested by the firefight. What will God's instructions be to you on that day? Fanciful theory? Impossible idealism? Infallible battle plan? Success or failure on the battlefield can hinge on how you've trained and prepared.

This section marks the halfway point through the longest chapter of the Bible, and it is without a doubt the emotional low point in the journey. The psalmist finds everything he believes about God tested to its limits. Can he hang onto righteousness when he's pushed past his breaking point?

81-82 I long for your salvation; I put my hope in your word. My eyes grow weary looking for what you have promised; I ask, "When will you comfort me? "

After putting all his hope in God, the psalmist watches time continue to pass while his situation stays exactly the same. The moment he thought deliverance would arrive came and went, and he's worn out. Have you ever found yourself in that same place? I think most of us have and will again many times over the course of life.

I'm grateful that the Bible gives us the honest truth about life's difficulty. Putting your hope in God doesn't mean denying reality. God doesn't ask you to pretend like what you're experiencing isn't painful. All throughout the Bible, God's people experience the lowest of the low. Some of them collapse under the pressure, but others push through and come out victorious on the other side.

83   Though I have become like a wineskin dried by smoke, I do not forget your statutes.

A dry wineskin no longer has the capacity to hold new wine. New wine expands as it ferments and would rupture the wineskin. Jesus used the same analogy in Mark 2:22. Here, the psalmist admits, "I'm no longer useful. I don't have the capacity to try anything new. I'm completely worn out."

What he does do is hang on. God's statutes are hidden in his heart, and rather than try a new solution, he hunkers down and goes all-in on where he decided to plant his faith long ago.

Have you ever noticed that when you've got a persistent problem, people seem to come out of the woodwork with suggestions? *Have you tried this? Have you looked into that? Do you know what I would do in your shoes?* People around you won't necessarily understand when you hold firm to God's Word when it doesn't appear to be working, but hold firm you must!

84 How many days must your servant wait? When will you execute judgment on my persecutors?

If you've ever watched a marathon, you will have observed that most of the runners speed up when they can finally see the finish line. There's something about seeing the destination that energizes them enough to push through the pain for those last few hundred meters. It's always easier to endure when the end is in sight, but what about when you feel like you're running blind? That's where faith must kick in. What you can't see in the natural, you must see in your spirit. Faith sees the Word of God fulfilled before it comes to pass in the natural. Lock your spiritual eyes on what God has promised, and keep running the race.

85 The arrogant have dug pits for me; they violate your instruction.

God will never violate His Word. The enemy, however, violates God's instructions all the time. When you experience a situation that runs contrary to the promises of Scripture, you can rest assured that God's not the one behind it. He is faithful and true. On the other hand, the devil looks for opportunities to rebel against God's sovereignty and pull you into losing your faith or, even worse, slandering God's character. These schemes are traps, deep pits that the enemy digs. Be careful not to fall into them.

In the 1560s, Queen Elizabeth was the sovereign leader of the British Empire, but a group of earls in the northern regions unsuccessfully attempted to overthrow her government and install Mary Queen of Scotts. They set out to defy Elizabeth's sovereignty, but they failed because Elizabeth had the power to back up her authority. She mustered England's army, who dutifully quelled the rebellion.[5]

In the same way, Satan's arrogant rebellion does not make God less sovereign. God has all authority, and He has all power to back it up. In His sovereignty, He has chosen to make those of us in Christ part of His means of advancing the Kingdom of Heaven into every place Satan opposes Him. This is why it is vital that you stay true, even when circumstances seem to violate God's instruction. God is still Sovereign, and He will be victorious no matter what. To participate in His victory, keep standing firm in Christ Jesus.

86   All your commands are true; people persecute me with lies -- help me!

No matter what the enemy throws your way, don't back down from God's Word. Satan is a liar, and since the beginning, he has desperately wanted people to believe that God is a liar like him. Some of the most painful wounds occur when Satan uses other people to attack you and spread his lies. But remember, God is always your helper, never your problem.

---

[5] Kesselring, Krista. 2021. "Participants In The Northern Rising (Act. 1569–1570)". *Oxford Dictionary Of National Biography*. https://www.oxforddnb.com/view/10.1093/ref:odnb/9780198614128.001.0001/odnb-9780198614128-e-95586.

כ kaph

87   They almost ended my life on earth, but I did not abandon your precepts.

The worst thing the enemy can do is kill your physical body, but God grants eternal life to those who do not abandon Him. When you take your last breath, it's not the end; it's just the beginning. Knowing that God has, once and for all, removed the sting of death, you can stand tall when the enemy threatens your life. The devil has nothing on you. He can never take away your obedience.

88   Give me life in accordance with your faithful love, and I will obey the decree you have spoken.

When the enemy threatens you with death, remember the goodness of God, and pray, "Jesus, give me life!" Then, continue to obey. Simple, steady obedience will overcome the devil's most malevolent schemes.

God's character is unwavering and purely good. Not only that, but He is always victorious. If you remain in Him, you will also always be victorious. When the fog of war settles on the battlefield, open the eyes of your heart and see the light of Christ. He is the light that shines in the darkness, and the darkness will not overcome it.

KEYS FOR STUDYING SCRIPTURE

1. Simple, steady obedience will overcome the devil's most malevolent schemes.

2. Satan is a liar, but God is always true to His Word. Always.

ל
LAMED

John, the beloved Apostle of Jesus, opens his Gospel with the grandest and most wondrous statement about Christ: "In the beginning was the Word, and the Word was with God, and the Word was God." Jesus embodies and identifies with the Scriptures in a way that is supernatural and mysterious. When read through eyes of faith, the Bible grants access to the real and living presence of God. Not everyone reads this way, and those who don't, just like the Pharisees and Sadducees who approached Jesus with cynicism, walk away with little to show for their encounter but a heart even more hardened. However, all who approached Jesus with awe and wonder received a touch from God Himself. Those who read the Bible this way receive the same.

89   LORD, your word is forever; it is firmly fixed in heaven.

This verse is one of the most crucial and powerful in the Bible, and one could write an entire book about it. It is the hinge upon which all of Psalm 119 hangs, written in the exact center of the chapter, as if to say, "Look here! Don't miss this!"

God's Word is settled in Heaven. It is established and fixed like an immovable pillar. The implications here are massive. God has set up His Word as the supreme law of the universe, and He gives it no expiration date.

God is sovereign and omnipotent. He is capable of doing anything, anywhere, any time, as He pleases. In His sovereignty, we must observe, God has chosen to establish His Word and fix it in place. Not only that, He has sovereignly chosen to be faithful and true to His Word at all times and for all eternity. Therefore, He cannot lie (see Hebrews 6:18, Titus 1:2). He will uphold His Word without fail. In a genuine sense, not only does God bind everything in the universe to His Word, He also binds Himself to it. He could have chosen any means of His liking by which to govern creation, and He decided to rest the total weight of His sovereignty upon His Word.

God's choice to be true to His Word makes Him accessible and reliable. By His Word, we are given the means to access His will and declare Heaven's perfect law over every circumstance. God's ears listen for people who will give the Scriptures the reverence they are due, and He moves in power for disciples when they access His promises by faith. This is why the psalmist frequently turns God's promises into his prayer and why Jesus taught the disciples to pray, "Your Kingdom come, your will be done on earth as it is in Heaven."

90   Your faithfulness is for all generations; you established the earth, and it stands firm.

Not a single Word God speaks ever fails to accomplish its purpose. If God spoke a promise 5,000 years ago, He will honor that promise today. No part of the Scriptures will fail. God will be faithful until every last detail has been fulfilled.

The force of God's Word is so powerful that it literally caused matter to come into existence when God commanded the earth to be formed. Everything He established will stand firm until His plan is completed to absolute perfection. It is impossible for God to say, "Let there be light," and not have radiant light burst forth in obedience to Him.

A widespread deception has crept its way from the fringes of Christian culture into the mainstream: that the Bible was written by a particular people within a specific cultural context and is therefore largely irrelevant, incapable of being literally true, and certainly not authoritative. This false doctrine aims to undermine the sovereignty of God, much the same as Satan has done since the beginning. The Bible is quite full of cultural context, such that any necessary details for proper interpretation are already found within its pages. Supplemental understanding of the historical, cultural context of the Bible may indeed be helpful to the reader. However, the Truth of God's Word (and the power God rests upon it) transcends all time and space. It supersedes all culture and historical context. For all generations, God is faithful to His Word.

If you took a man and raised him from birth into adulthood on an island with no knowledge of history or sociology and gave him a Bible without any supplemental training or resources, he would find in it everything necessary to live a powerful, righteous life, fully connected to God. Would sound doctrinal teaching and additional contextual knowledge be of use to him? Certainly. But even without them, God would be true to His Word and make available to this man the pathway to Salvation in Jesus, liberty from all bondages, and the miraculous power of every single promise written in its pages.

91   Your judgments stand firm today, for all things are your servants.

God is not the source of sin nor its evil, painful effects on your life, but He will employ it to your advantage for His glorious purposes. God is relentlessly redemptive. He is capable of taking everything that Satan intends for evil and using it for your good (see Genesis 50:20). All things, even the theft, death, and destruction of the enemy, will ultimately bend to His will as servants. Satan is playing checkers, and God is playing 3-dimensional chess. God is a strategic mastermind, constantly wielding the schemes of Satan against him, defeating darkness at every turn. When you rely on God's judgments, the vilest circumstances the devil throws at you will only work to your advantage. God is not the source of anything evil, but all things, good and bad, are His servants.

92   If your instruction had not been my delight, I would have died in my affliction.

As the last section indicated, the psalmist has traversed the deep and dark valleys of life. On the other side, he knows that the sustenance of the Word is what kept him alive. Even during deadly affliction, he calls God's instructions "delight." Likewise, God has stored up delight for your darkest hour to hold you secure when everything around you collapses. He has prepared a delightful feast for you in the presence of your enemies (see Psalm 23).

93 I will never forget your precepts, for you have given me life through them.

It would be easy enough to interpret this verse metaphorically, but the statement here is literally true. The psalmist just said in the previous verse that he would have died without God's instruction. God's Word contains supernatural power to impart life to a dying person. Jesus literally healed the sick and raised the dead with a word. That same supernatural power is available to you every time you open the Bible.

Don't forget this! Forgetting that God is supernatural causes us to look outside of Him for solutions to our problems. The seer-prophet Asaph wrote in Psalm 78 his retrospective diagnosis for what went so tragically wrong in Israel's history that they should find themselves in slavery all over again. He identified that one of the underlying causes of their great grief was that they forgot God's miracles and ceased to believe in His wondrous works. God is a miracle-working God, the same yesterday, today, and forever (see Hebrews 13:8).

94 I am yours; save me, for I have studied your precepts.

Scripture doesn't just give us the ability to know *about* God. It gives us the means to actually know Him. Knowing about God doesn't bring salvation, but knowing *Him* brings salvation and eternal life.

The psalmist not only studies about God but personalizes what he's read. The precepts he's come to understand from his study have become access points to God's goodness and generosity. His magnificent response to God is a declaration so powerful that it still saves lives today: "I am yours." Those words of total love and surrender are an eternal wedding vow to a Bridegroom King.

95   The wicked hope to destroy me, but I contemplate your decrees.

Don't be alarmed at the fact that the enemy wants to destroy you. Think about what God has decreed, and know that He always has the final say. For every wicked thing the enemy throws your way, God has already decreed its conclusion, and there's nothing that all the powers of darkness can do about it. Satan can never outwit, outlast, or outwork the power of God's Word.

96   I have seen a limit to all perfection, but your command is without limit.

God's Word is beyond perfection with zero limitations. It doesn't merely work up to a certain time period, after which you must find your own culturally relevant solution. It doesn't stop working after the scales have been tipped in God's favor, leaving you with a balance of mostly good. It doesn't work only for a special class of elite people. It doesn't cease after it's already benefitted you once before.

God's command extends beyond the limits of time, space, science, philosophy, and common sense. Nothing that the world considers elegant, beautiful, wise, admirable, certain, pleasing,

ל lamed

effective, comforting, true, or trustworthy even begins to compare with the inexpressible, limitless, flawless Word of God.

KEYS FOR STUDYING SCRIPTURE

1. God has sovereignly chosen to stand by every detail of His Word without limit or failure.

2. God is supernaturally present when we read His Word through eyes of faith.

3. The Word gives us access to know God, not just know about Him.

מ
MEM

As we have already observed, obeying God's commands is vital for a disciple's wellbeing. Study alone is not enough. Application takes Scripture from being informative to transformative. When we put the Word into practice, the Holy Spirit wraps our obedience in God's grace and transforms us from the inside out. The Holy Spirit helps us when our obedience is weak, informs us when our understanding is faulty, lavishes upon us the inheritance of Jesus, and convicts us of our true and righteous identity in Christ (see John 16:7-15).

Without action, what we get from Scripture is far worse than empty intellectual knowledge, for any time we know the right thing to do but don't do it, it is sin (see James 4:17). But every time we put the Word into practice, the wisdom of God saturates our character, and we experience the benefits of His brilliance applied to our lives.

97   How I love your instruction! It is my meditation all day long.

Around our kitchen, my wife and I have several favorite cookbooks that we return to again and again. We love cookbooks that have lots of pictures and personal details about the recipes from the chefs. Sometimes we go through them dreaming about what dish we should try next. We use them to plan meals and grocery lists. We learn about flavor combinations the recipes join together and think about which recipes might pair well with each other.

While there's plenty of enjoyment to be had just reading a well-written cookbook, all cookbooks are written to be put to use. Eventually, you must cook, or the book has done nothing but entertain your imagination. The best cookbooks not only teach you how to cook specific dishes but also teach you technique along the way, going beyond helping you successfully execute a meal to make you a better cook. Eventually, good cooks use what they learned in one recipe and apply the techniques to all kinds of dishes.

The Bible is very much like our favorite cookbooks. In its pages are a bountiful feast. The feast doesn't end when your Bible reading time is over but continues as you ponder it throughout the day and allow it to shape your worldview. What we learn through one life season always ends up being applicable during a different season. Our meditation on God's instruction keeps us nourished, even when we're not actively reading.

98   Your commands make me wiser than my enemies, for they are always with me.

One of the great benefits of God's Word is the wisdom it cultivates in a disciple's heart. God's Word can take a fool and make Him wiser than all His peers. Even a child who learns

Scripture will become astoundingly wise. When you fill your soul with the wisdom of Heaven, all of the enemy's schemes begin to fall flat against you because Satan can never outmaneuver God's intellect.

Biblical insight isn't just the kind of wisdom you find in a self-help book or personal growth seminar. It's supernatural. James 1:5 says, "Now if any of you lacks wisdom, he should ask God—who gives to all generously and ungrudgingly—and it will be given to him." This is a prayer I pray all the time, especially before reading the Bible. The Holy Spirit takes our time in the Word and uses it to transform our minds, pulling us into the majestic genius of our Creator God. When you close your Bible, the Holy Spirit remains with you, drawing your mind further into God's brilliant thoughts.

99 I have more insight than all my teachers because your decrees are my meditation.

Often, the world's teachers focus on addressing the symptoms of a problem without ever getting to the heart of the matter. Without knowing what God thinks about any particular issue, it's impossible to understand it truly. God's commands not only address surface-level symptoms but also help us gain insight into the root systems from which problems grow.

For example, there are lots of books on the market about overcoming fear. Most of them promote incremental courage, learning about your fear, positive visualization, or breathing techniques. However, any approach to fear that focuses on fear misses the root of the problem. 1 John 4:18 informs us that perfect love casts out all fear. Fear isn't the problem but the symptom of a soul that has not encountered God's perfect love.

Jesus always had brilliant insight! When the teachers of the law tested Him and tried to trap Him, Jesus saw through their deceit, straight to the heart. He was able to cut through the noise and silence their questions. God's decrees help us acquire and implement Heaven's insight into earth's problems.

100 I understand more than the elders because I obey your precepts.

Once again, we must emphasize that gaining knowledge by itself isn't enough. 1 Corinthians 8:1 warns that knowledge alone will puff a person up with pride. Merely knowing more than someone else can make you a know-it-all or an arrogant jerk. However, when we apply God's Word through loving obedience, we are built up into the character of Jesus.

101 I have kept my feet from every evil path to follow your word.

The psalmist here describes a proactive guard on his behavior to set himself up for success. Far too often, people want to know how close they can get to the edge of a cliff without falling off. How much can you indulge a temptation before it becomes sin? This is a dangerous game and entirely the wrong approach to righteousness.

Reverence for God's Word and proper understanding of His goodness always lead a disciple to go beyond the bare minimum. Others may sometimes misunderstand your behavior as legalistic when in reality, your motive is honor. But any price you might pay for righteousness is always worth it. The broad road of sin may look harmless and inviting at its outset, but it is steep and costly. Keep your feet firmly on the narrow path, and you will avoid the pitfalls of temptation.

102   I have not turned from your judgments, for you yourself have instructed me.

While dozens of different human authors penned the Bible, it isn't simply a collection of men's ideas about God. It is the Spirit-inspired Word of God Himself. He is the divine Curator, and He collected and preserved every word on the Scripture's pages intentionally for your instruction.

Furthermore, when you read your Bible, you need never read alone, for the Holy Spirit is with you and within you to teach you and counsel you. God Himself is your Instructor. The Scriptures are an open invitation to come and sit at the feet of Jesus, like Mary Magdalene, and learn from the Master.

103   How sweet your word is to my taste -- sweeter than honey in my mouth.

Put the Word of God on your lips. Let every word that comes out of your mouth be flavored with the sweetness of Heaven. Put the Scriptures into practice, and it will sustain you more than any meal. Jesus said, "My food is to do the will of Him who sent me," (see John 3:34). Obedience to God is a continual feast that nourishes your spirit, soul, and body. When confronted by the bitterness of life, look for ways to sweeten your thoughts, words, and deeds with God's Word. If you hunger and thirst for righteousness, you will be filled.

104 I gain understanding from your precepts; therefore I hate every false way.

Jesus issued the Pharisees a sobering indictment in John 12:43. "They loved human praise more than praise from God." The cares of the world, the praises of humans, the love of wealth, the lust of the flesh, the allure of power…all of these are false ways that lead to the same destructive destination. Be on guard against detours away from the straight and narrow.

Numbers 22-25 recounts the sad story of Balaam, a prophetically gifted man who very reluctantly obeyed God but kept his heart tangled up in the love of money and power. 2 Peter 2:15 describes him as "loving the way of wickedness." Eventually, Balaam's insincere obedience caused his complete destruction.

A disciple must learn to love what God loves and hate what God hates. God loves people, but He hates the sin and compromise that destroys them. Make sure to gain understanding from your obedience, and don't just obey begrudgingly. God has a loving purpose for all of His instructions. You won't always understand it on the front end, but as you obey, seek God's understanding of the situation. If you miss God's heart behind His commands, you will find yourself repeating Balaam's folly.

True discipleship leaves no room for "agreeing to disagree" with God. We must reform our thoughts and learn to think like God thinks. All of His ways toward us are rooted in perfect love and limitless insight. It takes humility to yield your opinions and experiences over to God, but when you do, the Holy Spirit will lead you into the glorious path of God's insight. Nothing He does is cavalier. All God's precepts are seeds of supernatural wisdom that blossom into a life sweet and fragrant with His loving kindness.

KEYS FOR STUDYING SCRIPTURE

1. Putting the Word into practice brings supernatural knowledge, wisdom, and insight.

2. Begrudging obedience leads to compromise and sin. As you study and obey, pursue God's loving heart behind His commands.

ב

NUN

_ _ _

ore than just true in a philosophical sense, the supernatural power of God makes the Word miraculous to anyone who puts it into practice. As we have discovered, this power isn't met without resistance, but for the faithful disciple, the force of God's Word is unstoppable against any obstacle. When you put the Word to work, the Word works.

105   Your word is a lamp for my feet and a light on my path.

Jesus said in Matthew 6:22-23, "The eye is the lamp of the body. If your eye is healthy, your whole body will be full of light. But if your eye is bad, your whole body will be full of darkness. So if the light within you is darkness, how deep is that darkness!" Continuous study and practice of God's Word fills you with light. The light of the Word fills your entire being with the presence and power of God.

Many have described the "lamp for my feet" as a small light that only makes the next step visible, which may be valid for particular seasons of life. However, the Scriptures provide so much more to us than a dim glow. Jesus said, "You are the light of the world. A city situated on a hill cannot be hidden. No one lights a lamp and puts it under a basket, but rather on a lampstand, and it gives light for all who are in the house. In the same way, let your light shine before others, so that they may see your good works and give glory to your Father in heaven" (see Matthew 5:14-16). Inaction will keep your light dim, hidden under a basket, but obedience will fill your life with glorious light, bright enough to outshine all of Satan's darkness.

106   I have solemnly sworn to keep your righteous judgments.

In the Old Testament, it was common for a person to swear an oath of allegiance to God. The only problem with this practice was that people often found themselves unable to keep their oath and under the weight of punishment for their failure. Jesus elevated the disciples' view of commitment to God in Matthew 5: "let your 'yes' mean 'yes' and your 'no' mean 'no.'"

Jesus perfectly kept all of God's righteous judgments. By faith, we are enveloped into Jesus' perfection and perfectly kept in Him. Through the miracle of salvation, we no longer take an oath to righteousness but die completely to unrighteousness. Where we once would fail to uphold such oath, Jesus fulfilled all righteousness. The sin that once made us wretched is now buried in the grave, and our new man is raised to life in Christ's flawless holiness. Our commitment to obedience is now a response of gratitude and faith.

107   I am severely afflicted; LORD, give me life according to your word.

The Word of God contains the promise and power of life. Whether your need is physical, spiritual, or emotional, God has stored up life within the pages of Scripture. We can be confident even through the harshest affliction, God will not withhold His goodness from us.

Studying the promises of God will prepare you for a day of trouble. Memorizing Scripture gives your faith an anchor when storms try to knock you off course. Don't be caught off guard but prepare for your journey with a ready supply of Truth. During severe affliction, remember that God has given you His solemn Word that He will bring you life.

108   LORD, please accept my freewill offerings of praise, and teach me your judgments.

Every trial is an opportunity to give God a special offering of love and praise. In Heaven, for all of eternity, the pain and affliction we experience will be erased forever. This means that only now, in this life, do you have the opportunity to offer God worship through trouble and suffering[6]. It's easy to praise God during a season of celebration, but when you freely give God praise during hardship, you give Him a gift that is precious and costly. It is an offering that is fragrant and wonderful to Him.

Throughout the Psalms, you'll notice a pattern of praise and worship, even in the middle of the worst circumstances. This kind of praise helps us keep a keen view of God's goodness and recognize that God's character is not compromised through grief

[6] See the chapter "The Wilderness" in my book *Monuments of Grace* for more on this topic.

and trouble. Praising God through adversity positions your heart in gratitude for God's answer even before breakthrough happens.

Faith and gratitude are inseparably intertwined with each other. When Jesus healed ten lepers, and one of them came back to say, "thank you," Jesus responded to him by saying, "Your faith has saved you." Jesus received the man's thanks as an offering of faith. Hebrews 11:1 tells us, "Now faith is the reality of what is hoped for, the proof of what is not seen." When we praise before we've seen what we hope for come to pass, we engage in the kind of faith that moves mountains!

109-110 My life is constantly in danger, yet I do not forget your instruction. The wicked have set a trap for me, but I have not wandered from your precepts.

The enemy's trap is always set off-course from God's way, but he is powerless to defeat you if you don't wander astray. Ultimately, Satan wants to draw your allegiance away from God and turn your heart from Him. He does this by provoking you with attacks and difficulties, but all his schemes are temporal and temporary. Jesus' victory, on the other hand, is eternal.

Jesus warned the disciples. "Don't fear those who kill the body but are not able to kill the soul; rather, fear him who is able to destroy both soul and body in hell." Know that Satan's trap is to use earthly assault in an attempt to lure you off the pathway to the Kingdom of Heaven. He is powerless to force you off the straight and narrow, but he schemes to make you feel powerless to stay on it. Nothing could be further from the truth. In Christ, you are perfectly kept, and God will not allow you to experience temptation greater than you can bear (see 1 Corinthians 10:13).

Throughout history, militaries have kept detailed war plans containing strategic maneuvers for every conceivable contingency. These plans help commanders make crucial decisions during conflict, avoiding confusion and costly mistakes. The Bible contains all the battle plans you need for facing your spiritual enemy. Reliance on God's instructions without wavering will keep you safe from danger and out of the devil's traps.

111 I have your decrees as a heritage forever; indeed, they are the joy of my heart.

God's decrees are an inheritance of incalculable value. In Christ, you share the entire inheritance of Jesus. Everything that He earned by living a perfect life has been passed on to you, his co-heir. Even in the places where you've fallen short of keeping God's decrees, you inherit Jesus' steadfastness. His victory, His righteousness, and His eternal fellowship with the Father are all rightfully and legally yours. He earned it, and He bestowed His heritage onto you. This is an inheritance worth celebrating!

112 I am resolved to obey your statutes to the very end.

Obedience has no expiration date. Every backup plan to God's way of doing things is an idol. Idols divide your heart and mind and rob you of experiencing the goodness that God has stored up for you. James 1:6-7 describes a double-minded person as being like an unmoored vessel battered and tossed by the waves: "That person should not expect to receive anything from the Lord." What a terrible trap to fall into! It is critical that disciples become single-minded about the Word of God.

Resolve to follow God's statutes no matter what. Fix your gaze on Jesus, our bright beacon, our straight and narrow road, our glorious destination. Study the Scripture, and treasure it in your heart. Let the Word illuminate your pathway from the inside out, and follow His light all the way home.

KEYS FOR
STUDYING
SCRIPTURE

1. Turn the promises of God into praise, even before breakthrough happens.

2. Resolving in advance to keep God's commands can keep you from straying into Satan's traps during conflict.

SAMEK

On any given subject, cultural influences shape and sway people's opinions. Surrounding each of us are differing combinations of family culture, peer group culture, church culture, popular culture, political culture, etc. These influences may either reinforce or detract from what God's Word says about an issue, and to the degree that they disagree, a disciple's position is necessarily counter-cultural. While disciples should always love their families, friends, and country, our loyalty is first and foremost to a King and a Kingdom. Even church culture and Kingdom culture do not always align. Kingdom culture is the perfect implementation of "Thy will be done on earth as it is in Heaven." The culture of Heaven is worship expressed wholeheartedly in thought, word, and deed.

There is great danger in merely incorporating Christian ideas into your existing way of life. Jesus cannot only be an influence. He must be the supreme Lord of every aspect of life. Baptism into Jesus means the death of our old life, our previous way of thinking, and our past patterns of behavior. When Jesus is taken merely as an addition, He cannot truly be Lord, and we are rendered double-minded by default. As we saw in the previous section, the great danger of being double-minded is that we "should expect nothing from God (see James 1:6-7)." Being of one heart and mind is of utmost importance because a divided heart and mind always siphons away faith and leads to compromise.

113   I hate those who are double-minded, but I love your instruction.

The takeaway here (especially for New Testament disciples) is not to hate people but to hate double-mindedness. The Old Testament finds its fulfillment in Jesus, and the New Testament shows us the pathway forward in Him. Jesus said that the Scriptures speak of Him (see John 5:39), and therefore we must look to Jesus and what He set in motion to understand God's Word. We must always interpret the Old Testament through the greater revelation found in the New Testament, not the other way around. That being said, Ephesians 6:12 tells us that our struggle isn't "against flesh and blood, but against the rulers, against the authorities, against the cosmic powers of this darkness, against evil, spiritual forces in the heavens." Our enemies are not other people but the forces of evil that enslave them and the spiritual strongholds that keep people in captivity.

Double-mindedness is a cold, dark prison that keeps people from experiencing God's goodness. Double-mindedness divides our faith between God's outcome and something else (which is inevitably less than God's best). Our mission is to be single-minded about God's instruction. Everything God says is true, and we can't afford to have competing thoughts with His. King David prayed this impactful prayer in Psalm 86:11, "Teach me your way, LORD, and I will live by your truth. Give me an undivided mind to fear your name." We must choose to set aside our opinions and the opinions of others and learn to treasure God's instruction.

114 You are my shelter and my shield; I put my hope in your word.

Those who put their trust in God's Word will be sheltered from the storms of life and shielded from the enemy's attacks. The waves that batter the double-minded to their breaking point are rendered powerless by the mind and heart firmly fixed on God's decrees. God never gives false hope. He is a trustworthy sanctuary for those who put their trust in Him.

115 Depart from me, you evil ones, so that I may obey my God's commands.

It is a fact of life that the people we surround ourselves with have tremendous influence on our behavior. Choose your friends wisely, and don't entrust your heart to people who live disobedient lives. Of course, this doesn't mean withholding grace and compassion from people. After all, Jesus spent significant amounts of time with sinners. However, it does mean denying the disobedient a position of influence in your life, which can sometimes be a lonely road. It's better to be isolated and obedient than surrounded by company and compromise God's instruction.

When following God's ways means walking alone for a season, God will always be your faithful friend and companion. He knows better than anyone the friendship and community that your heart desires, and He will not deny you what you need.

116 Sustain me as you promised, and I will live; do not let me be ashamed of my hope.

It was God's sovereign choice to stake His reputation on keeping promises, and He will never fail to keep His Word. When you feel weak and unable to carry on in faith, ask Him to be your sustainer. Not only is He faithful towards you, the Holy Spirit works His faithfulness through you from the inside out. He will provide life to every part of you that feels hopeless and exhausted. Through the Holy Spirit, God pours into us the steadfastness of Jesus, who stood victorious at the end of every trial and temptation. This is the supernatural, empowering grace of God.

117 Sustain me so that I can be safe and always be concerned about your statutes.

God will never put you in a position that makes obedience impossible. No matter how precarious your situation is, God has always crafted an escape from evil. If your heart is committed to His righteousness, He will alert your eyes to see the way forward every time. He will sustain you through what feels like impossible circumstances. With the Holy Spirit as your Helper, there is no temptation or hardship that you cannot endure (see 1 Corinthians 10:13). No situation can remove His presence from you. Keep your eyes fixed on Him, and He will uphold you.

118-119   You reject all who stray from your statutes, for their deceit is a lie. You remove all the wicked on earth as if they were dross from metal; therefore, I love your decrees.

God is holy and perfect. Imperfection cannot survive in His presence. That's why Jesus paid the ultimate price to cover you and transform you with His perfection. Nothing outside of Christ can provide you the ability to stand in God's presence, no other religious path nor even your own ability to keep God's instructions. However, inside of Christ, you are no longer defined by imperfection but transformed into the very righteousness of God (see 2 Corinthians 5:21). When all is said and done, God's ultimate commandment is to embrace and obey Jesus (see John 3, John 14:6, Matthew 17:5). Every other pathway is a lie that leads to destruction.

120   I tremble in awe of you; I fear your judgments.

God is worthy of our utmost reverence. The fear of the Lord is like a diamond that refracts God's light in different ways depending on the angle from which we view it. Outside of Christ, the fear of the Lord can be pure terror, as we see in the many Biblical accounts of God's enemies being struck with panic when they encountered His presence. However, for those of us in fellowship with Jesus Christ, the fear of the Lord becomes awestruck reverence for His holiness and glory. It is to be overcome with

God's worth and power, all the while confidently fixed in God's goodness.

On a recent hiking trip with my nieces and nephews, we ventured up a mountain in the Ozarks to a lookout spot that jutted out from the rock over the valley below. The view was nearly 360 degrees around, spectacular and breathtaking. However, as each of us took in the beauty of our surroundings, we were deeply aware of the edge of the cliff where we stood, careful that our footsteps were secure and mindful of the great height. There was no horseplay among us at the top of the cliff because we were respectful of our position and attentive not to fall. The fear of the Lord is in many ways similar, as we simultaneously experience the beauty of God's unfathomable goodness and tremble at His majestic power. We are simultaneously immersed in perfect peace and trembling fear, knowing that in the Father's love, all that power exists for our benefit and is opposed to anything that might harm us.

Proverbs 9:10 tells us that the fear of the Lord is the beginning of wisdom. It is the anchor that keeps us single-minded. In Him, we don't vacillate between competing realities. Whatever the culture we live in presents as truth must always remain yielded to what God says is true. For the world, truth constantly changes and evolves, but God is constant, unwavering, and unyielding to outside pressure, forever good and righteous. Yielded to Him through Christ, all of His mighty judgments work in our favor. God Himself is our anchor and safe harbor through the stormiest sea.

samek

KEYS FOR STUDYING SCRIPTURE

1. **Double-mindedness robs people of experiencing God's goodness.**

2. **We study God's Word to become single-minded about His truth for our lives and the world around us.**

3. **Being anchored in Christ and His truth shelters us through all of life's storms.**

ע
AYIN

W oven into every fiber of your being is the ability to commune and fellowship with God. God Himself exists in perfect community and harmony, three in one: Father, Son, and Holy Spirit. You were created in His likeness, born for unity and relationship with Him. Jesus' prayer for you is that you would be one with the Father, the same way He is (see John 17:21). Outside of Christ, our ability to abide in God is completely cut off and dead, but through Jesus' atoning sacrifice, we are once again grafted into the source of eternal, abundant life.

Our position in God is secure through every circumstance, and our ability to communicate with Him is inseparable from who we are. We were born for relationship with Him. Whatever the season, regardless of challenges, we don't pray from a position outside of God trying to get in. He is inside us, and we are inside Him. He is above, below, all around, and within. Communion with God is our default at all times.

121   I have done what is just and right; do not leave me to my oppressors.

In Ephesians 4:26-28, the Apostle Paul warns against giving the devil (through sin, bitterness, and anger) an opportunity to harass and oppress you. Legally speaking, Satan has no right to oppress you, for all authority has been given to Jesus (see Matthew 28:18). All of the devil's work is illegal. However, just because a thief has no legal right to enter your home and steal your possessions doesn't make it a good idea to leave your doors and windows unlocked and open. Don't give the thief an opportunity!

Whenever you find yourself facing oppression, it's always a good idea to pause and assess whether there's any sin in your life that has given the enemy opportunity to harass you. Invite the Holy Spirit to convict you of any area of your life where you have fallen short of God's ways. He will always do so with compassion and lovingkindness. If there is sin to deal with, the solution is simple and readily available. All you need to do is repent and turn away from that sin towards God. As we mentioned before, repentance is firstly agreeing with God about the nature of your problem and turning your thoughts, words, and deeds away from your ways to His. His mercies are always new and available to you. The Holy Spirit will empower you to keep God's ways, and the blood of Jesus will keep you in His righteousness. Repentance closes and locks your doors and windows, keeping the thief out.

Perhaps you've already done this, yet you still find yourself being harassed. Like the psalmist, your prayer is, "God, I have done what is just and right!" Rest assured that God is your protector and your defender. He will not permit injustice to reign in your life. Stay steady, and be confident in God's victory.

122   Guarantee your servant's wellbeing; do not let the arrogant oppress me.

Isn't this prayer wonderful? I love the psalmist's confidence in God's protection. Would you be courageous enough to pray for God to *guarantee* your wellbeing? I promise you God loves this kind of prayer. He does because it demonstrates your attentiveness and acceptance of His promises. It shows that you really believe what He has said about Himself and what He says about you. Guarantee your servant's wellbeing, oh God! The oppressor doesn't stand a chance.

123 My eyes grow weary looking for your salvation and for your righteous promise.

Where else do you turn when your eyes grow weary looking for God's promise? It would be a mistake to divert your eyes to another possible remedy. Any solution available to you outside of God's promise is a mirage. Perhaps it looks satisfying to a thirsty soul, but in reality, it's deception that will lead you far off course and leave you even more parched.

Another option is to fixate on the problem, a trap many of us fall into, but you can't solve oppression by staring at oppression, sin by studying sin, nor fear by gazing at fear. Staring at the problem only enlarges the problem, feeding it with worry and anxiety.

Instead, when you are weary, waiting for God's salvation, look to Jesus Himself. He is salvation. He is both the Promise and the Promise Keeper. He is strength for your weariness. Psalm 121 says, "Where will my help come from? My help comes from the Lord, the Maker of Heaven and earth."

What you look at during times of trouble makes a massive impact on the outcome of your situation. The Apostle Paul gave wise counsel in Philippians 4:6-9: "Don't worry about anything, but in everything, through prayer and petition with thanksgiving, present your requests to God. And the peace of God, which surpasses all understanding, will guard your hearts and minds in Christ Jesus. Finally brothers and sisters, whatever is true, whatever is honorable, whatever is just, whatever is pure, whatever is lovely, whatever is commendable -- if there is any moral excellence and if there is anything praiseworthy -- dwell on these things. Do what you have learned and received and heard from me, and seen in me, and the God of peace will be with you."

Look to Jesus. Ponder His goodness. Pray for His promise with thanksgiving in advance, and the God of peace will be with you. He is more present than your trouble. He is never separate. Jesus is with you always.

124   Deal with your servant based on your faithful love; teach me your statutes.

Did you know that your perception of God impacts both your behavior and how God deals with you? Jesus told a parable about three servants entrusted with the same responsibility, each receiving money to look after while their master was away. Upon the master's return, two servants had wisely invested the money and grown what was entrusted to them. The third, however, was afraid of what would happen if he lost money, and he opted to hide it rather than invest it, simply returning to the master what belonged to him. Here's what happened (from Luke 19:20-24):

ע ayin

"And another came and said, 'Master, here is your mina. I have kept it safe in a cloth because I was afraid of you since you're a harsh man: you collect what you didn't deposit and reap what you didn't sow.' He told him, 'I will condemn you by what you have said, you evil servant! If you knew I was a harsh man, collecting what I didn't deposit and reaping what I didn't sow, why, then, didn't you put my money in the bank? And when I returned, I would have collected it with interest.' So he said to those standing there, 'Take the mina away from him and give it to the one who has ten minas.'"

Because the servant thought poorly of his master, he squandered the opportunity to manage well what was given to him. The servant's fears rendered his actions into self-sabotage, and the master was left unable to reward the servant's laziness. What would have happened had the servant perceived his master as a generous rewarder of a diligent worker? How might he have behaved differently? In the end, it wasn't the master's character that was the servant's undoing but his own actions. He ended up not being a servant at all.

In the same way, when we correctly perceive the perfect character of God, it causes us to follow His statutes with diligence and aim our faith at His goodness. God always stands ready to deal with us on the basis of His faithful love, but often our actions cause us to deal with Him on different terms than His own.

A significant part of learning God's statutes is learning the character of our Teacher. As you study Scripture, a good question to ask is, "What does obedience look like in light of God's goodness?" Hebrews 11:6 says, "Now without faith it is impossible to please God, since the one who draws near to him must believe that he exists and that He rewards those who seek Him." God is not a harsh master but a loving Father who rewards our diligence. Viewing Him correctly positions us to receive the reward of faithful servants and loving sons and daughters.

125 I am your servant; give me understanding so that I may know your decrees.

The sequence here is important. We must never place understanding *before* obedience, but we must also not neglect to seek understanding as we obey. Refusal to obey before understanding is simply disobedience. A good soldier doesn't violate an officer's commands just because he doesn't understand the battle strategy. However, a diligent soldier will study the commander's strategies and grow along the way.

Often it's impossible to understand what God is up to on the front end of obedience. However, God honors the surrendered heart and shares with us His wisdom as we step out in faith and obedience.

126 It is time for the LORD to act, for they have violated your instruction.

The psalmist once again prays an unimaginably bold prayer. He has grown confident in God's perfect justice. He knows that wherever injustice occurs, God always moves in to make things right. On our side of the cross, we can be doubly confident that God is working all things for our good, for Jesus has paid in advance the price to make right every injustice we face. When is it God's time to act? 2 Corinthians 6:2 says, "See, now is the acceptable time; now is the day of salvation."

127-128   Since I love your commands more than gold, even the purest gold, I carefully follow all your precepts and hate every false way.

God's desire for us has always been relational. He isn't a harsh task-master who wants compliance based on manipulation and control. The correct foundation for obedience is love. When we see Him as He truly is, He's easy to love! Jesus flawlessly demonstrated that God the Father isn't a harsh master, waiting to punish the servants who are unsuccessful. No! He rewards our faith in Him with His own success.

You were born for relationship with God. He delights in you. He enjoys spending time with you, sharing His unfathomable wisdom and insight. For sons and daughters of God, knowing the love of the Father makes obedience more valuable than any substitute the world has to offer. We honor God not because He's scary but because He's wonderful. His plan for you is better than you can fathom.

KEYS FOR
STUDYING
SCRIPTURE

1. Scripture provides us an honest mirror to examine our behavior.

2. Repentance and grace draw us from sin back into to God's perfect standards.

3. Our understanding of God's character greatly impacts our obedience.

4. Love for God is the most secure foundation for obedience.

פ

PE

The more we put the Word of God into practice, the more we experience the Kingdom of Heaven. When God's laws become our foundation, His government becomes our protection and supply, and everything about His world is superior to the natural world. Obedience, therefore, is not tedious or legalistic. It's a joyful adventure with God as our guide, our companion, and our destination.

129 Your decrees are wondrous; therefore I obey them.

The decrees of God unlock signs and wonders. Every miracle of Jesus was rooted in His obedience to the Father (see John 5:10). When He speaks, universes and galaxies are formed! When we obey His commands, we position ourselves to be on the receiving end of His miraculous power.

After spending time with Jesus, his disciple Peter latched onto the power of Jesus' commands. When he saw Jesus walking on the water, Peter wasn't content to remain a spectator. Earlier that day, he had seen how Jesus' command healed the sick and how his blessing multiplied food. So Peter calls out to Jesus with a radical idea:

"Lord, if it's you," Peter answered him, "command me to come to you on the water." He said, "Come." And climbing out of the boat, Peter started walking on the water and came toward Jesus" (see Matthew 14:28-29).

Peter knew that if Jesus commanded him to walk on water, he would be able to walk on water. And so he did. Peter actually sought out a command to obey! That's how wondrous God's decrees are!

130   The revelation of your words brings light and gives understanding to the inexperienced.

Just a few short years after walking on water with Jesus, Peter stood on trial before the Sanhedrin, the same judicial body that turned Jesus over to be crucified. Obedient to Jesus' commission, Peter and John ministered healing to a lame man at the entrance to the temple, and the Sanhedrin were furious at them for claiming Jesus had been resurrected from the dead. Who were these men? They weren't educated scholars like themselves. They were only fishermen! Yet Peter and John had an undeniable quality about them:

"When they observed the boldness of Peter and John and realized that they were uneducated and untrained men, they were amazed and recognized that they had been with Jesus. And since they saw the man who had been healed standing with them, they had nothing to say in opposition." (see Acts 4:13-14)

Peter was uneducated and untrained, but He had *been with Jesus.* Jesus revealed light and understanding about the Word of God that the Sanhedrin had no access to outside faith in Him. We don't obey God in a vacuum but in the revelation light of Jesus Christ.

If you were to read a job listing for disciples in the newspaper's classified section, in big bold letters, it would say, "Workers needed to do the impossible...no experience necessary." When we obey Jesus and follow in His footsteps, we step into His experience. The same Holy Spirit who was present with Jesus for every single miracle He performed is present with you. He has all the experience and revelation you could possibly need.

131   I open my mouth and pant because I long for your commands.

Are you beginning to understand why someone would long for God's commands? God does not issue commands to heap burdens upon you but to set you free. He longs to walk with you and work on your behalf. Every command is an opportunity to step into God's world and reap the benefits of His miraculous ways.

When you study the Word, look diligently for the commands of God. Search for His decrees. Find out what He has to say about your family, your finances, your health, your time, and your aspirations. Yielding these to God through obedience opens the floodgates of Heaven to you. Seek His Kingdom and His righteousness, and His world will begin to invade your yours, setting you free from worry and fear (see Matthew 6:25-34). God's commands make the crooked path straight. They level mountains and build up valleys. They shine light on what is dark and obscure.

132   Turn to me and be gracious to me, as is your practice toward those who love your name.

What does it mean to love God's name? The psalmist isn't saying He likes the phonetical sound of God's name when he pronounces it. God's name is His seal of authority. When the United States Congress passes a law, it doesn't carry any legal authority until the President signs it, and only the President's name can take that piece of paper and make it the law.

Knowing and experiencing the goodness of God draws us out of rebellion. In His world, rebellion brings weakness, but submission brings strength. God's regular practice is to be gracious towards you, and this makes it easy to submit to His authority. When you understand His character and observe His actions, God's name is easy to love.

133   Make my steps steady through your promise; don't let any sin dominate me.

God will never leave you too weak to obey Him. He's too good for that. You never have to be afraid of failure because God does not require you to obey Him in your own strength. When we submit to Jesus, we gain access to the same power that enabled Him to resist all sin. As we grow in our character, even when we sin and fail to keep God's command, we remain kept inside His promise to sustain us. All that He requires of us is to repent and carry on in obedience.

The old man who was once a slave to sin, unable to resist the desires of this world, is dead and gone, buried with Jesus in the waters of baptism. The new man is clean, powerful, and favored by God. Nothing about you now is defined or identified by sin, for you have exchanged this old identity for God's righteousness. When you walk in yielded submission to Him, it is impossible for sin to dominate you. He won't let it happen.

134   Redeem me from human oppression, and I will keep your precepts.

In the truest sense, God has already fulfilled this request of the psalmist. Jesus is our eternal redemption from all oppression. No person, nor demon, nor sickness, nor circumstance can prevent you from keeping God's precepts. God will uphold you through any trial and empower you through any pressure. The grace of Jesus will not fail you.

135   Make your face shine on your servant, and teach me your statutes.

Jewish readers would be very familiar with the phrase, "Make your face shine," for it was the blessing that Moses taught the priests to pronounce over the nation (see Numbers 6:23-26). It is a blessing of God's favor, protection, and peace. The psalmist knows that the better he learns God's statutes and walks in them, the more he avails himself of God's blessing. But God's blessing is more than physical or circumstantial; it is His very presence—to stand before Him face to face. The presence of God is both the reason for our obedience and the means by which we obey. To stand in the light of God's face is to be empowered, to have every need fulfilled, to be perfectly protected, and to be completely at rest.

136   My eyes pour out streams of tears because people do not follow your instruction.

God's heart for the disobedient is one of immense compassion. These tears are the tears of someone who has tasted of God's goodness and experienced His mercy. The psalmist knows what it's like to be disobedient yet forgiven and welcomed home by a merciful King. He knows firsthand the empty pleasures of disobedience and the satisfying bliss of following God's ways. Those who disobey harm themselves, for they deprive themselves of the warm glow of God's glorious face.

A lifestyle of obedience means stepping into the culture of God's heart, and He sacrificed everything to draw the disobedient back into companionship. Diligent disciples of Jesus must embrace the compassion Jesus has for the lost. In Luke 15, Jesus describes the disobedient in three parables, each using language of value and love. To God, the disobedient are lost sheep, lost coins, and lost children, worth weeping over until they are found.

KEYS FOR STUDYING SCRIPTURE

---

1. God's decrees unlock signs and wonders. When reading Scripture, search for what God has decreed.

2. Obedience positions us to experience the benefits of God's wonders.

3. Scripture helps us learn God's compassionate heart and how to respond to people like He does.

צ

TSADE

W hy do we obey God? We've spent considerable time in our journey through Psalm 119 talking about the necessity of obedience and the many benefits of it. In some sense, we follow God's commands because it would be foolish not to. The abundant provision God makes for the obedient and the perils that lay outside of God's ways make obedience the only rational choice. However, obedience isn't only about advantage. Behind the many benefits of obedience is a person: God Himself.

We obey God because obedience is a part of worship. We worship God because, in every way, He deserves it. Worship is more than the songs we sing at church before the preacher delivers the sermon. Worship is our response to who God is and what He has done through our thoughts, words, and deeds.[7] In its purest form, obedience is simply a disciple's reply to the magnificent perfection of God.

137 You are righteous, LORD, and your judgments are just.

---

[7] I wrote extensively about the lifestyle of worship in my book *Monuments of Grace*.

God is right about everything. In all things, He is morally superior. God has never, not for a moment, been unjust. Nothing He has ever done is merely satisfactory; everything He does is exemplary. His motives are entirely pure. His outlook and insight are unblemished. He has never been wrong. He has never fallen short of what He set out to accomplish. He is entirely righteous.

138   The decrees you issue are righteous and altogether trustworthy.

Emanating from a righteous and trustworthy God are righteous and trustworthy decrees. God's commands and His character are not separate from each other. For this reason, Jesus is identified as the "Word made flesh."

As New Testament disciples, even the parts of Old Testament law that we no longer practice serve as type and foreshadowing of what Jesus brought to fruition. Much of the Old Testament was focused on the concept of consecration, being set apart for holiness. In Christ, we find the fulfillment of those ideas, as we are set apart in Him and made holy by Him. When the Old Testament laws were in place, they perfectly demonstrated the righteousness of God, our dire need for His mercy, and His steadfast goodness in spite of our disobedience.

Having been set apart and made holy by Jesus, the law we follow is still anchored in what God established in the Old Testament: "Love the Lord your God with all your heart, with all your soul, with all your strength, and with all your mind," and "your neighbor as yourself" (see Luke 10:27). In other words, love God with all your convictions, emotions, actions, and intellect; and love others the way you desire to be loved. All of our obedience is rooted in how Jesus demonstrated these commandments to us. He is righteous and altogether trustworthy.

139   My anger overwhelms me because my foes forget your words.

Everything that happens outside of God's decree is unrighteous and unjust. The psalmist's anger here is righteous, hating what God hates. Remember, the New Testament informs us that our "foes" are not other people but the spiritual forces of Satan that influence and draw the world into sin (see Ephesians 6:12).

Righteous anger never leads to anxiety, fear, impatience, or anything outside the fruit of the Spirit (see Galatians 5:22-23). Instead, righteous anger compels disciples into action to advance the Kingdom of God wherever we see the enemy at work. This action takes many forms: prayer, evangelism, and even caring for the physical needs of others. Regardless of how we engage with our foes, we have the Word of God and all its promises on our side.

140   Your word is completely pure, and your servant loves it.

The more trouble the psalmist finds himself in, the more he leans into the goodness of God. Satan loves to sow seeds of doubt about the purity of God's Word. He has done so from the beginning, and we see the evidence of this all throughout culture today. Opponents of God constantly twist the Scripture or try to frame it against their own distorted sense of morality, accusing God of being unjust, hypocritical, and hateful. But neither God nor His Word are any of these things. He is entirely pure and deserving of our love, as are the Scriptures.

141 I am insignificant and despised, but I do not forget your precepts.

You may be insignificant and despised in the world's eyes, but in God's eyes, nothing could be further from the truth. His value for you is unmatched by anything in the universe. God's precepts serve as evidence of His value for you. By His perfect law, you have become His adopted son or daughter, and there is no higher identity to obtain. The world cannot reject you, not really, because God has already accepted you.

142 Your righteousness is an everlasting righteousness, and your instruction is true.

Have you ever noticed that the morality of the world changes at an alarming rate? To see this in action, watch a sitcom from 20 years ago and compare its morals to pop culture today. Many times, my wife and I have sat watching an old TV show and said, "This would never air on TV today." What was once considered moral and acceptable is now an abomination, and what was once unthinkable is now celebrated openly. Not so with God. He is constant and unchanging. He has always been and always will be righteous. Since the beginning, we partake of and participate in His righteousness by faith. He is utterly reliable and unchanging.

143 Trouble and distress have overtaken me, but your commands are my delight.

Begrudging obedience will eventually wear out. This is why we must carefully seek to understand God's heart behind His commands. Discovering the purity of His commands, we find that His instructions are not a burden but a delight. If at first you don't find one of God's commands delightful, learn to adjust your perspective and seek understanding from the Holy Spirit. After all, He's right about everything and only has good things in mind. Keep obeying, and look for God's goodness in what He has instructed.

Don't let trouble and distress overtake you. Obey God with a joyful heart, and He will see to it that your trouble and distress are vanquished.

144 Your decrees are righteous forever. Give me understanding, and I will live.

Jesus said in John 8:31-32, "If you continue in my word, you really are my disciples. You will know the truth, and the truth will set you free." We don't obey God from a position of impoverished obligation, trying to obtain freedom through our own efforts. Instead, we have come to know the Truth, that is Jesus Christ who is the Truth, and He has made us free. Obedience flows from His righteousness, and the unfathomable riches we find as we obey all flow from His perfect character.

Psalm 119

Throughout Christian history, there have been some teachers who stray into doctrinal error through legalism while others stray into error by overemphasizing the immense prosperity God makes available to His children. One side fails to understand how lavishly God desires to bless us, and they rob themselves of opportunities for thanksgiving. The other side fails to see how worthy Jesus is of total sacrifice, and they deprive themselves of opportunities to worship. Both of these extremes come from the same error: they do not fully comprehend the righteous perfection of God. God is so incalculably good that He would deserve our obedience even if it were of no benefit to us whatsoever. At the same time, He is also so immeasurably wonderful that it's impossible to exaggerate how staggering His benefits are for us.

We obey because of Him, for He is altogether magnificent.

KEYS FOR STUDYING SCRIPTURE

---

1. We obey Scripture because God is righteous, completely deserving of our loyalty.

2. The entirety of Scripture demonstrates God's perfection.

3. Recognizing God's righteousness leads to joyful, enduring obedience.

ק
QOPH

Jesus never demonstrated passive endurance of Satan's evil. 1 John 3:8 says that Jesus' mission on earth was to "destroy the works of the devil." Being a disciple of Jesus, you are commissioned to join Him in that work. Romans 16:20 says, "The God of peace will soon crush Satan under your feet." In other words, God's method for bringing peace to your life is to crush Satan in the tread of your footsteps.

When challenged directly by Satan in the wilderness, Jesus didn't rely on His own experiences but instead turned to the Scriptures. For every new temptation Satan brought, Jesus countered with, "It is written…" The Bible provides us with both offensive and defensive weapons against every scheme of the enemy. If the thought of spiritual warfare makes you nervous, take heart. Every battle we fight is waged from the position of victory Jesus already won on the cross. Through His Word and the power of the Holy Spirit, God provides every weapon you will ever need for the fight. Are you ready for battle?

145   I call with all my heart; answer me, LORD. I will obey your statutes.

Wholehearted reliance on God is a position of absolute strength, not one of weakness. The world values self-reliance, but self-reliance always leads to self-destruction. There is no pathway to strength outside of Godly surrender. We can be confident that God hears us when we cry out to Him, for He wholeheartedly supports us. He will always answer, never leaving you to languish hopelessly. As you wait for His answer, resolve to obey, no matter what God might ask of you. In the meantime, obey what you've already been instructed. Don't delay and make your obedience conditional on future circumstances. Faithful obedience will lead you into God's provision for any situation.

146   I call to you; save me, and I will keep your decrees.

After God brings breakthrough, don't stop obeying. It's a common mistake to lose one's fortitude once the pressure is off, but be determined to stay faithful through both the valley and mountaintop. We must depend on God and remain loyal to His commandments whether we are in lack or abundance, in sickness or perfect health, surrounded by friends or entirely alone. All too often, people turn to God only when things are going poorly and forget about Him when all is well. No relationship can thrive on those terms. Instead, we must use answered prayer as fuel to carry on in Him, growing ever deeper in love and devotion.

147   I rise before dawn and cry out for help; I put my hope in your word.

ק qoph

Be diligent and intentional in prayer. Rising before dawn is a sign of discipline and dedication, a preemptive step that precedes any challenges the day might bring. Here, prayer is connected to the Word, which provides an anchor of true hope at all times. Turning the Word of God into prayer is a reliable way to connect to God's victory, for His decree will never fail.

Remember, you have not been sent into the fray alone. Jesus has sent the Holy Spirit to be your Helper (see John 14:26). Imagine it! The Creator of the Universe has come to offer you His assistance at all times. It's like having Rembrandt help you paint or Einstein help you with your math homework. The Holy Spirit makes available to you all the wisdom and power of God. How could we not avail ourselves of this great gift by asking for help before we begin the day?

148 I am awake through each watch of the night to meditate on your promise.

During any challenge, remember to keep watch for God's promises instead of fixating on the problem. Set your heart and mind on what God already decreed about the outcome and wait with great anticipation for it. The psalmist's picture of staying up all night meditating on God's promises is one that says, "Any minute now, breakthrough is coming. It must because God has promised it." Don't be caught unaware when God comes with His victory, but train yourself to be attentive and alert, always looking for Him. Instead of waiting passively, look for ways to participate in His promises. Throughout Scripture, you will observe breakthrough coming to those who serve diligently as they wait. Jesus is the Promise Keeper. Anticipate Him with joyful expectation.

149 In keeping with your faithful love, hear my voice. LORD, give me life in keeping with your justice.

Prayer should always be offered on the basis of God's character. Taking your eyes off of God's perfection may cause you to falsely assume that God is your problem instead of your helper. Prayers that misjudge God's character miss their mark. Basing prayer on something outside of God's complete goodness is double-minded by default and seldom effective. Thankfully, God is merciful and good, whether you realize it or not. All too often, whether overtly or subtly, our prayers end up communicating, "God, I need help, but at this moment, You're failing me." He is not failing you, not even for a second.

The seer-prophet Asaph provided us tremendous insight in Psalm 73 about what happens when pain distorts our view of God, "When I became embittered and my innermost being was wounded, I was stupid and didn't understand; I was an unthinking animal toward you. Yet I am always with you; you hold my right hand." While God is gracious and can handle your anger, you must know that anger aimed at Him is always off target. Ask Him to take your hand and lead you to a higher vantage point where you can see both Him and your pain as they truly are. God is your defender, not your enemy. He never deprives you of justice but always makes things right. He sympathizes with your pain more than you could imagine, and He's the only one who can truly bring healing.

150 Those who pursue evil plans come near; they are far from your instruction.

Take note of how the enemy violates God's instructions, for this is precisely why they will be defeated. Nothing can stand in opposition to God. Whenever Satan violates God's statutes by robbing, killing, and destroying, the God of Justice is on your side. Study the Word to know your rights as a citizen of God's Kingdom and a member of His family. Don't tolerate it when the enemy tries to steal what Jesus paid for with His righteous sacrifice, and stand firm on the laws of God. Never be afraid when the enemy comes near. Remember that God is a righteous judge, and Jesus is your legal advocate. The court is stacked in your favor.

151 You are near, LORD, and all your commands are true.

However near the enemy might be, God is always nearer. The Holy Spirit has taken up residence inside of you, and He doesn't bring only a small portion of God's nature with Him. He puts the fullness of God that is in Christ Jesus inside of you. Colossians 2:9-10 says, "For the entire fullness of God's nature dwells bodily in Christ, and you have been filled by him, who is the head over every ruler and authority." Christ in you stands in absolute authority over all, and He is your constant guardian.

God has never given a command under false pretenses. His commands are trustworthy and reliable. As you read Scripture, search for what God has spoken about your protection, your wellbeing, your provision, and your family. Praying in agreement with God's commands positions you at the center of His will, and His will for you is unwaveringly good.

152   Long ago I learned from your decrees that you have established them forever.

The longer you walk with the Lord, the more you will experience His goodness. When times are difficult, drawing to remembrance the many ways that God has been faithful in past seasons will bolster your faith for the fight at hand. From cover to cover, the Bible recounts stories of God's decrees coming to pass, even long after people had lost hope. Regardless if you're new to your walk with God or a seasoned veteran, remember that God already paid the ultimate price to save you; He won't leave you to languish now. He's already given you everything and will not withhold what you need. So, stay in the fight, and don't be discouraged.

The Apostle Paul writes in 2 Corinthians 10 about the spiritual battles we face. We don't fight using natural means but through the powerful spiritual weapons God equips us with. Paul says, "We demolish arguments and every proud thing that is raised up against the knowledge of God, and we take every thought captive to obey Christ." What does it mean to "take every thought captive"? It means that we don't allow our minds to spiral into thoughts that disagree with what God decreed in His Word. We don't allow any idea to compromise the truth about God's goodness. God's decrees supersede our circumstances, experiences, and our opinions. His goodness is always intact, regardless of our vantage point in any situation.

ק qoph

Knowing what God has commanded and promised is a vital part of engaging in battle with the enemy. The Word trains us to be single-minded and full of faith about the outcome of a situation before it happens. God's perspective is much too valuable to ignore. His side is always the winning side. The more you learn to walk in His ways and stand on His promises, the more of His total victory over Satan you will experience. Align yourself with Jesus. He never loses a battle.

KEYS FOR STUDYING SCRIPTURE

1. Scripture is an effective weapon for spiritual warfare.

2. Wholehearted surrender to God is the most powerful position you can take in any battle.

3. Be resolved to obey before, during, and after any trial or crisis.

4. Learn your rights as a citizen of God's Kingdom and a member of His family, and don't tolerate the enemy's theft.

⅂
RESH

ndurance is a persistent theme throughout the New Testament. In Revelation 2 and 3, Jesus gives incredible promises to "the one who conquers" and "the one who keeps my commands to the end." At the same time, He issues stern warnings to anyone who strays from the faith and compromises God's instruction: "I know that you have persevered and endured hardships for the sake of my name, and have not grown weary. But I have this against you: You have abandoned the love you had at first. Remember then how far you have fallen; repent, and do the works you did at first." In both our actions and heart motives, we must endure in the love that Christ Jesus gave us.

At this point in the psalm, it might be easy to think of what's written as repetitive, but repetition in Scripture is intentional. Biblical writers use repetition for emphasis and to help the reader remember what's important. The story of Jesus' ministry, for example, is so crucial that it appears in four different books written by four different authors, each giving us a unique vantage point from which to examine Christ's life and character.

The psalmist finds himself continuing to battle opposition, but the repetition here demonstrates to us what faithful endurance looks like even through lengthy trials. After all that he's battled, he continues to hang on to what he's learned from God's Word.

153 Consider my affliction and rescue me, for I have not forgotten your instruction.

Notice that affliction hasn't caused the psalmist to lose sight of God's Word. Knowing that God is a just and loving God, he appeals to His compassion for rescue. Let's not forget that all Scripture points us to Jesus (see John 5:39). Though the enemy's attack may be ferocious, we must remember that God's rescue is promised, and in the greatest sense; it has already happened through Jesus' death and resurrection.

Every affliction in life is only temporary, but Jesus' rescue is forever. However, that doesn't mean that we should delay our hope into a time that we have no access to in this life. Don't fall into the escapist mindset that you must wait for either death or Jesus' return to experience victory. If you're facing trials in this life, God is still the God of breakthrough in the here and now. God knows that deferred hope makes the heart sick (see Proverbs 13:12), and He doesn't dangle false hope in front of His children. Instead, we should contend for a victorious outcome right now, knowing that God has provided us a win/win as long as we don't abandon our faith.

154 Champion my cause and redeem me; give me life as you promised.

How can you be certain that God will champion your cause? When you pursue the Kingdom of Heaven and hold fast to God's instruction, God will always back you up. Sadly, many people want to live on their own terms but expect God to rescue them when they get into trouble. God cannot champion a cause that opposes His. We must learn His priorities and make His cause our own.

155 Salvation is far from the wicked because they do not study your statutes.

Receiving the benefit of God's Word requires faithful study and application. Salvation can't be found anywhere outside of God's way, and studying the Word reveals that God's way is the person of Jesus Christ. He is the Way, the Truth, and the Life. No one approaches God except through Him. My accomplishments can't help me, nor can my own sense of morality, my own convictions, or my own attempt to right my wrongs. God's command is to receive the lordship of Jesus Christ. To the one who studies and obeys God's statutes, salvation is not just near, it has already come.

156 Your compassions are many, LORD; give me life according to your judgments.

Once again, the psalmist lays his request on the foundation of God's love and just judgment. To say that God is compassionate is to acknowledge that He sympathizes with our pain and weaknesses and cares enough to act on our behalf. God is not aloof or apathetic towards His children but is always ready to move on our behalf.

To see God's compassion in action, we need only look to Jesus. Compassion is the defining motive for everything that Jesus did. Whether it was healing the sick, raising the dead, multiplying food, or teaching people about the Kingdom of Heaven, whenever a motive is listed, it's compassion. If you are in Christ, God's judgment towards you is always life-giving and favorable.

157 My persecutors and foes are many. I have not turned from your decrees.

Despite facing betrayal, abandonment, persecution, and even death, Jesus never wavered from completing His mission to break the curse of sin and death over the world. All twelve disciples ran away from Him. The Roman government's justice system was a complete farce that wronged Him in every way. The religious leaders accused Him of being demonized and demanded His execution. The crowds chanted in agreement. His captors mocked Him and beat Him beyond recognition. Yet through all of this, Jesus remained true and did not turn from God's decree. In every way, Jesus is our model for how to faithfully walk out Scripture.

158 I have seen the disloyal and feel disgust because they do not keep your word.

Disobedience to the Word not only hurts others but hurts the disobedient as well. God despises sin because it disfigures His image He crafted in each of us when He created us. Sin breaks our fellowship with Him. Having every right to destroy us in our rebellion, God instead moved in compassion to make all things right again. Rather than leave us in sin's distortion of our identity, Jesus became physically disfigured and restored us to the likeness of our Father.

We too should ache in disgust when we see sin's effects on people's lives, but we should never let that disgust interfere with our compassion and value for lost people. Instead, we lead them to Jesus, whose grace and mercy do not fail, regardless of how heinously we've broken ourselves.

159 Consider how I love your precepts; LORD, give me life according to your faithful love.

Remember that God is a rewarder of those who diligently seek Him (see Hebrews 11:6). It's not that we have anything to add to Jesus' perfection, not at all. However, God is so gracious that He counts Jesus' faithfulness as our own while also counting our own faithfulness as worthy of reward. He never lets your obedience go unnoticed because He's far too generous for that.

160 The entirety of your word is truth, each of your righteous judgments endures forever.

As much as Satan has tried to undermine the truth of Scripture over the centuries, he fails at every turn. God's Word is supernaturally enduring and empowers us to endure in Christ. As we faithfully study and apply His righteousness to our lives, God's judgments continue to work on our behalf.

When you find a passage of Scripture that you don't understand or that troubles you, don't lose heart. Look to Jesus for understanding because He is the Word Made Flesh. He demonstrates to us how to live as citizens of God's Kingdom. For every place that sin pushes humanity down into the dirt, God's judgment uplifts those who entrust themselves to Christ and follow Him. When trials and persecution ramp up, stay steadfast. Look to Jesus, who is your strength to endure. You can do all things in Him.

KEYS FOR STUDYING SCRIPTURE

1. Repetition is used in Scripture for emphasis and to help us remember what's important.

2. Jesus is our model for how to walk out Scripture.

3. In both the Old and New Testament, look for how Jesus fulfills what is written. The entirety of Scripture speaks about Him.

SHIN

The length of Psalm 119 gives the reader an opportunity to journey with the psalmist through his life and observe his continual response to God, even as the circumstances around him change. What we find is that the Word of God transforms him as he faithfully puts it into practice. We have followed him through the joy and excitement of walking with God: "How happy are those who walk according to the Lord's instruction!" We've grieved with him when the emotional floor collapsed beneath him: "My life is down in the dust." Ultimately, he discovers that, while seasons continually change and his emotions may pivot and waver, God's Word is steady and utterly reliable. Setting his foundation on God's constancy has transformed him from the inside out. What used to cause him despair no longer does. Even though trials persist, he is now bold and fearless.

Throughout your life, change is unavoidable. As you experience joys and sorrows, your character will be shaped and molded one way or the other. Without the Word as your foundation, you will inevitably find your life warped by fleeting happiness and metastasized trauma. However, when you submit your life and experiences to Christ and allow His Word to define you, you will journey into a Kingdom where joy is a foundational pillar of the culture and there is true healing balm for every trauma. The Holy

Spirit will use the Word to fashion your life into one that looks like Jesus.

God's Word is transformative, but we must yield to that transformation. As the psalmist has done, despite pressures and temptations to give up, stand firm and let the Word of God define your character, settling for nothing less than God's decree. In Him, you'll find true and lasting redemption, identity, and purpose.

161 Princes have persecuted me without cause, but my heart fears only your word.

Most people in the world are shaped and motivated by their fears. Without God, it's impossible to live unaffected by fear. This fall from God's security began as soon as Adam and Eve ate from the forbidden tree. After disobeying, they immediately cowered and hid from God. Without the abiding love of Jesus transforming our nature, we can't help but fear life, God, other people, losing control, not having enough, being alone, being misunderstood... Outside of Jesus, the list of things to fear is endless. Ungodly fear is submission to anything other than Christ's love. Whatever you fear has power over you. The more we resist and struggle against the pressures of this world without God's sovereignty ruling our lives, the more we end up being shaped by them.

The sole cure for fear is total submission to the One who gives us no reason to be afraid. Fearing God is the only way to find true security because He is the only One worthy of such reverence. As we submit to Him, God transforms our fear from anxiety and terror to awe and wonder. In Him, all other fears are rendered powerless because His power is on our side.

162　I rejoice over your promise like one who finds vast treasure.

The Apostle Paul wrote in Philippians 4, "Rejoice in the Lord always. I will say it again: Rejoice!" The promise of happiness that the psalmist began with has become his reality. Rather than make his joy dependent on what's going on around him, he has discovered that God's promises are always with Him, unchanging and ever-powerful in effect. He no longer waits for his trials to end but instead rejoices his way through them. In the Kingdom of Heaven, we are never without reason to rejoice because everything we do is rooted in Jesus' character and total victory over evil. With Christ our Joy, we have continual reason to rejoice.

When you learn to read the Bible like a treasure hunt, the Word becomes an inexhaustible source of joy. Proverbs 25:2 says, "It is the glory of God to conceal a matter and the glory of kings to investigate a matter." Having been adopted into the royal family of Jesus, you have the kingly privilege of hunting for the extravagant riches of His glory. He does not hide anything to withhold from you but because the search itself grows you into His strength and character. Reading the Bible without treasuring God's promises is like using a gold bar as a doorstop. Hiding the Word in your heart uncovers the treasure He has hidden.

163　I hate and abhor falsehood, but I love your instruction.

Lies are the native tongue of Satan's kingdom (see John 8:44). Even when something he says sounds true, you can be certain that it's coated in poison. God's instruction, however, is our plumb line (our laser level, if you will) for evaluating what's true and what's false. Make no agreements with falsehood, partial truth, or tantalizing opportunities to ignore the truth.

When we read the Word of God, it's crucial that we don't approach it with the intent to prove ourselves right. Even Satan tried to twist Scripture out of context to benefit himself (see Luke 4:9-10). We must always give God permission to change our perspective with His Word. The Gospel doesn't validate you, it transforms you. God's vantage point on every subject is higher and better than our own, and when we read to validate ourselves, we miss out on understanding His ways. Instead, we must exchange our views and opinions for His, for only His are true.

164   I praise you seven times a day for your righteous judgments.

When trouble arises, praise God, because He already has determined the solution. As you read and discover His promises, praise Him, for the judgment is already in your favor. As you wait for breakthrough, praise Him, for He is your sustainer through every circumstance. If the situation seems hopeless, praise Him, because He is your Living Hope. When breakthrough comes, praise Him, because He is always true to His Word. When you look back on the journey, praise Him, because He never left your side. When you face the next trial, praise Him, because every trail is a new opportunity to grow in the knowledge of God and experience His faithfulness.

165   Abundant peace belongs to those who love your instruction; nothing makes them stumble.

Passages of Scripture that use words like "nothing," "all," "every," "always," and "never" provide us with clarity and trustworthy assurance. These are promises that you can lean your full weight into. So, search for them as you read, for they will help you grow single-minded. There is no reason to worry about stumbling when you love God's instruction. Even if you err, He won't allow you to fall and break but will gently instruct you back onto the right path. If you resist the Word of God, you will eventually find your way into anxiety and strife, but when you love God's commands, your peace will be unshakable. With God holding you up, nothing can make you stumble.

166 LORD, I hope for your salvation and carry out your commands.

Nothing is more reliable than God. If you obey His Word, submitting yourself wholly and completely to Him, there is no chance whatsoever that you might miss out on His salvation. All other foundations are quicksand. But obedience to Him makes you immovable. Jesus says in John 12:50 that God's command is eternal life. There is no life outside of Him, only death. But inside of Him is eternity. Faithful obedience occurs within hopeful expectation. When you place your hope upon Jesus, the Living Hope, carrying out God's commands comes with confident optimism.

167 I obey your decrees and love them greatly.

Obedience is an act of love and faith. When all is well and we can clearly observe the benefits of obedience, it's easy to follow God's Word. However, our test comes when we experience pain, when obedience is costly, and when we can't yet see the outcome of our circumstances. During uncertainty is actually when obedience is the most vital.

God can handle all of your questions. Unlike people, God does not become insecure when you ask Him about tough subjects. He has a brilliant and loving answer for all of them. Even so, it is important that your questions don't compromise your obedience. Oftentimes, God's answer to your question will become evident as you obey. To withhold obedience because your questions haven't been answered is simply rebellion, and rebellion hinders your ability to relate to God and hear His voice. Without His voice, you stand little chance of having your questions answered at all. Satan is always prowling about, happy to step in with a sugar-coated lie to take the place of God's truth.

The more we know God and understand His ways, the more wonderful His decrees become to us. Having faith in His unblemished character strengthens us to obey commands that don't make sense in the moment.

1 John 5:3 says, "For this is what love for God is: to keep his commands. And his commands are not a burden because everyone who has been born of God conquers the world. This is the victory that has conquered the world: our faith." Without obedience, we cannot honestly say that we love God or have faith in Him. Loving God's commands is inseparable from loving Him.

168 I obey your precepts and decrees, for all my ways are before you.

Obedience doesn't happen inside a vacuum. Whether or not we realize it, God always observes and participates in our lives. Disobedience prohibits us from receiving God's full abundance because He is incapable of violating His own Word. He cannot bless anything that His Word forbids. When we don't keep God's ways, we shouldn't expect to see His ways work on our behalf. Faithful obedience, on the other hand, never goes unacknowledged or unrecorded. Remember, God rewards those who diligently seek after Him (see Hebrews 11:6).

We do not belong to ourselves. Acting independently from God inevitably renders us wretched and inhuman, far from the "very good" creation that God designed us to be. Jesus paid the ultimate price to destroy our wretchedness and restore us to the beauty and purity of God's original design. All of your ways are before God, so let all of them reflect love for Jesus and gratitude for His immense love for you.

KEYS FOR
STUDYING
SCRIPTURE

1. Read the Bible like a treasure hunt for God's promises.

2. Don't read Scripture to validate your own viewpoint but to learn and adopt God's.

3. Allow God's Word to transform your thoughts, words, and actions. God is in the business of transformation.

TAW

Jesus is the Alpha and the Omega, the Aleph and the Taw. He is the beginning and the end. All things were created through Him, and everything is being reconciled to Him. All Scripture is inspired by Him, and all of it finds its fulfillment in Him. Without Jesus, Scripture would not exist. Without the testimony of Jesus, the Bible would be a book of unanswered questions, unfulfilled promises, and unresolved conflict. Jesus is both the foundation and the pinnacle of all revelation, wisdom, knowledge, and insight.

If you're reading the Bible for the very first time, I encourage you to start with Jesus. Read the Gospels and soak in the narrative of Jesus' life. Everything else in the Bible must be read through the lens of what Jesus revealed to us about God, the world, and His Kingdom. Without Jesus, Psalm 119 would be fruitless prayers and wishful thinking; but with Jesus, Psalm 119 gives us a key for unpacking Scripture in a way that glorifies Him and helps us fulfill our mandate as disciples.

Read this final section of Psalm 119 with Jesus in mind. Jesus is the answer to the psalmist's prayers. In Him, everything that Psalm 119 prophesies is fulfilled, even into your life this present day.

169   Let my cry reach you, LORD; give me understanding according to your word.

God promises that those who ask for understanding will receive it. For many, reading the Bible is a daunting task for which they feel unqualified. Sadly, throughout Church history, many leaders have agreed with this premise and tried to keep Scripture only in the hands of a select few. Thankfully, God raised up reformers and translators who have made the Bible available in nearly every language for disciples to study themselves. At great cost, brave men and women have labored over centuries to keep the integrity of Scripture intact and distribute it further and wider than any other work of literature in history.

By reading alone, even the wisest and most intelligent person in the world cannot possibly understand and receive the life that God promises us in the Word. Only Jesus provides the true key to understand and benefit from the Word. During Jesus' time on earth, the Jewish leaders were the foremost scholars of Scripture, yet in John 5:38-40, Jesus issued them a startling indictment:

"You don't have his word residing in you, because you don't believe the one he sent. You pore over the Scriptures because you think you have eternal life in them, and yet they testify about me. But you are not willing to come to me so that you may have life."

Only by embrace and submission to Jesus can the Word of God bring its benefits to the reader. In Christ, we have access to all the wisdom, insight, and power of God's Word, and the Holy Spirit helps us understand and practice what we read. Jesus is the fulfillment of the psalmist's prayer for understanding. As the Apostle Paul wrote in Colossians 2:3, "In him are hidden all the treasures of wisdom and knowledge."

170 Let my plea reach you; rescue me according to your promise.

God promises to rescue us, and the fulfillment of that promise is in Christ alone. The Pharisees and Sadducees were well acquainted with God's promise of a Savior, yet because they rejected Jesus, they also rejected the accomplishment of God's promise. There is no other rescue from the curse of sin and death besides Jesus. Many look to other rescuers, but all of them provide false hope. Some try to rescue themselves, but that is as foolish as trying to flap one's arms in order to fly. In Jesus alone, our rescue is secure.

171 My lips pour out praise, for you teach me your statutes.

Jesus has not left us alone to decipher the mysteries of Scripture. He freely gives the gift of the Holy Spirit, who is the most magnificent Teacher. No other teacher in the world can truly open his students' minds and make them able to understand the deep things of God, but Jesus can! Jesus takes little children and gives them more understanding than any adult can have on their own. Jesus takes the fool and makes him wiser than any scholar.

If you struggle to understand Scripture, praise Jesus in advance for opening the eyes of your understanding. When He gives you wisdom and insight, praise him with your thoughts, words, and actions. Let worship and praise be your constant response to the Teacher.

172   My tongue sings about your promise, for all your commands are righteous.

Even before you see a promise fulfilled, put the promise on your lips and sing! Literally sing! God deserves your voice and your song, and no one else can give it to Him. The praise and worship leader at your church cannot give the Lord your song. Regardless of your musical abilities, Jesus loves the melodies from your lips, and He deserves to hear them. You can rest assured knowing that, even as you sing, God goes about working all things together, fulfilling every detail of His promise. He is forever righteous and true and will never break His Word.

173   May your hand be ready to help me, for I have chosen your precepts.

In the face of persecution and death, the saints in Acts 4:29-30 echoed the psalmist's prayer. "And now, Lord, consider their threats, and grant that your servants may speak your word with all boldness, while you stretch out your hand for healing, and signs and wonders are performed through the name of your holy servant Jesus." Don't be afraid! As you boldly obey and proclaim the Gospel of Jesus Christ, God's hand is always ready to back you up in power. Choose Jesus and His precepts, and He will faithfully and supernaturally aid you as you fulfill the great commission.

In Mark 16:15-18, Jesus promised that as we obey Him, His hand would work on our behalf, "Go into all the world and preach the gospel to all creation. Whoever believes and is baptized will be saved, but whoever does not believe will be condemned. And these signs will accompany those who believe: In my name they will drive out demons; they will speak in new tongues; they will pick up snakes; if they should drink anything deadly, it will not harm them; they will lay hands on the sick, and they will get well."

The question you should ask yourself is not, "Will God really work these miracles through me?" He is always faithful to His Word. Instead, you should ask, "Will I obey His commands?" Choose His precepts, and walk them out diligently, and God will do what only He can do. Faith is not measured in what you can understand but in how you obey.

174 I long for your salvation, LORD, and your instruction is my delight.

Without the saving and empowering grace of Jesus Christ, God's instructions are a never-ending toil, a burden that cannot be shouldered. But in Christ, the burden of God's instruction becomes easy to carry as the Holy Spirit supernaturally empowers us for every task God assigns. Jesus ushers us into the ultimate Sabbath rest, and from His rest, we obey. We no longer labor to accomplish rest, but rest is our starting place from which we accomplish everything. The curse that Adam's sin brought upon the earth was broken at the cross, and obeying God's instructions is now truly our joy and delight.

175 Let me live, and I will praise you; may your judgments help me.

For all who receive Him, Jesus' judgments are life and liberty. We no longer need to cower under the fear of judgment because

God's verdict is in our favor. Jesus spoke of this favorable judgment in John 16:8-11 as He promised the Holy Spirit's coming: "When he comes, he will convict the world about sin, righteousness, and judgment: About sin, because they do not believe in me; about righteousness, because I am going to the Father and you will no longer see me; and about judgment, because the ruler of this world has been judged."

If you didn't read the entire passage in context, the thought of the Holy Spirit convicting the world about sin and judgment would be terrifying indeed! However, the Holy Spirit's conviction of sin leads us straight to Jesus. In Him, the Holy Spirit now proclaims a steadfast conviction of righteousness to our hearts. Judgment is no longer fearful because it is not us but Satan, "the ruler of this world," who has been judged. Praise King Jesus for His perfect judgments! His judgments help and do not hinder, and they are truly worth celebrating.

176 I wander like a lost sheep; seek your servant, for I do not forget your commands.

In the conclusion of Psalm 119, we see the clearest prophetic picture of Jesus. Though we, like sheep, wander astray, Jesus the Good Shepherd seeks and saves us. No matter how lost we have become, the Shepherd places us on His strong shoulders and carries us home to safety. This is what sets Jesus apart from all other gods. Every other religion gives followers a pathway to achieve their goal: peace with God, peace with themselves, peace with the world. All other gods give people instructions on what they must do to draw near. But Jesus does the opposite: He tells the world what God did to draw near to us. Seeing that we are hopelessly incapable of finding our way home on our own, the

ת taw

Good Shepherd left comfort and safety behind and pursued humanity to the ends of the earth. He is the Way home, and He finds us.

Jesus continually calls out to us, and He promises that we will know the sound of His voice. Every time you read the Word of God, the Shepherd's voice calls out to you. Listen, follow Him, and He will guide you into everlasting liberty and abundant life. How happy are you when you walk in God's instruction!

Psalm 119 is God's key to unlock Scripture, and Jesus is the One who holds that key in His hand. Only He can give it to you. What He opens, no one can shut, and what He shuts, no one can open. Come to Him and ask, and He will open the eyes of your understanding.

The psalmist has taught us many ways to engage with Scripture, treasure its wisdom, and reap its abundant benefits. Be faithful to put what you have learned into practice, and you will have a lifetime of encountering God through the study of His Word. You can never exhaust the living water of God. Jesus is truly the Word Made Flesh, and He is a well that will never run dry.

KEYS FOR
STUDYING
SCRIPTURE

1. All of Scripture is inspired by Jesus and finds its fulfillment in Him.

2. When reading Scripture for the first time, start with Jesus. He is the answer to all the psalmist's prayers.

3. Jesus holds the key to Scripture in His hand. He is the one who unlocks it and gives understanding.

ABOUT THE AUTHOR

Wes is a passionate disciple of Jesus Christ. He and his wife Hannah live in Nashville, Tennessee, with their border collie in a little house with a yellow door. Wes is a gifted speaker, writer, and worship leader. He has spent nearly two decades traveling the world building and empowering the global church, and he serves faithfully as a teacher and leader in his home church in Nashville.

For more information about Wes or to invite him to speak at your church or event, visit wespickering.com

Made in the USA
Columbia, SC
03 September 2021

44710596R00102